THE UNSPOKEN WORD

Epic Poetry

Anthony KaDarrell Thigpen

Library of Congress Cataloging-in-Publication Data

Anthony KaDarrell Thigpen
KaDarrell@sbcglobal.net
Literacy in Motion Publications

The Unspoken Word

ISBN: 978-0-9904440-7-7

1. Poetry – Epic, Spoken Word
Printed in the United States of America

Published by
Literacy in Motion
PO BOX 7186
Chandler AZ 85246
posttribune@hotmail.com

DEDICATION

My beloved, beautiful and intellectually brilliant wife of 10 years, Clara, who pushed, inspired, and encouraged me to release a revised edition of this book, *The Unspoken Word*. I love you passionately and unconditionally! This book was initially published in 2001, nearly 15 years ago, and every poem continues to capture time in a capsule of rhetorical expression.

My amazing, gifted and talented daughter, Amber Kindness, "I love you unconditionally, unequivocally, and inexplicably, you are Daddy's girl, and I am forever your best friend. You are the best of all that has ever come from me.

"My heart is inditing a good matter: I speak of the things which I made touching the king: my tongue is the pen of the ready writer. Thou art fairer than the children of men: grace is poured into thy lips: therefore God has blessed thee forever" (Psalms 45:1-2).

TABLE OF CONTENT

THE UNSPOKEN WORD

Anthony KaDarrell Thigpen

The Introduction

- *The Rising Velvet Curtains*

Chapter I

- *Interpretations*

Chapter II

- *Faces Of Reality*

Chapter III

- *Eight Shades Of Brown*

Chapter IV

- *That Thing Called Love*

Chapter V

- *Behind The Stained Glass*

INTRODUCTION
The Rising Velvet Curtain

As the author of *The Unspoken Word*, my desire is to poetically document the realities concealed within unspoken truths. My writing style reflects the traditional characteristics of epic poetry. Epic poetry consists of long narratives celebrating episodes of life. This literary composition possesses a dramatic overtone in order to place emphasis on important subject matter – such as despair, love, race, politics, and religion. My choices of words are often radical, unshaken, thought provoking, and grammatically arranged to reach people who lack exposure. The most valued aspect of this book is the added insight provided through biblical and modern life inspirations. The words unveiled within this book are anointed, life changing, and filled with passion. Poetry is a form of art; *The Unspoken Word* uses images from the human mind to allow individuals from a variety of different backgrounds to embark upon a common experience. Your interest has blessed me with the ability to share my gift with the world.

Poetry is my gift from God; *The Unspoken Word* is my gift to mankind.

Collisions

Certain rhetorical decisions,
Are limited by "politically correct" provisions,
But I speak with a violent impact –
In fact,
I'm unraveling
Dazzling –
Metaphoric collisions,
Carefully listen –
To me as I unveil unspoken thoughts,
Caught –
In fragments of short stories;
My poetry is epic,
The proper characteristic,
For this kind of intrusive deliberation,
I make no insinuations;
Each time I exhale,
My mind expels –
Exact –
Facts.

I only dialect in metaphors,
Leaving your –
Spellbound-craving mind
Wanting and longing,
For –
More and more,
Enthralled addicted minds,
I'm leading those who are spiritually blind –
To a world where reality is not imprisoned
Within the matrix of time.
I'm drawing and crossing –
The thin fine line in the sand,
Mentally I'm taking every man –
To the sublime.
I'm destroying the shackles of time,
And crossing over into eternity –
God's property.

Urban poetry,

Is the ability –
To exercise,
Without telling lies,
Your First Amendment right
Of freedom of speech,
The spoken word has the power to teach,
Because it can reach,

Across any societal breach –
From racial segregation,
To the missed education of Lauryn Hill,
Can you already feel –
Me aggressively and intellectually,
Causing your carnal mind to surrender to a greater will.

That's why philosophers call me deep,
Because when I speak,
My lyrics creep –
On tiptoes in the small corners of your mind,
I leave no space or time,
For false prophets and,
Imitational poets to read between the lines.
I've taken the English language,
Tied it up like a hostage;
I'm changing it,
And rearranging it.

I'm talking about urban poetry –
The power inside in of me,
Which unveils human frailties,
Digs deep within the imagination,
Then speaks freely without abbreviations,
Eliminates the hesitation.

I'm a Christian brother,
So why should I stutter,
Because another
Mortal man,
Disagrees with what I'm saying.
My words get radical,
Because that is all

It takes –
To make a difference.

I have the power of life and death
Lingering on the tip of my tongue,
This is my life-story and my theme song.

I live in a world where we inhale
Micro-diabolical particles,
Therefore, I exhale lyrical expressions,
Which teach explicit lessons,
About reality, liberty, and spirituality.
Divine knowledge nibbles on my earlobe,
Then I climax and mind explodes.
Taste me and see –
That I'm the salt of the earth,
My spoken words are worth,
More than ancient rubies,
Because if you knew me,
You would come correct,
And know that I'm worthy of,
And give me the respect,
That great black minds deserve.

Because I'm opening your mind with precise incisions,
Making life threatening decisions,
Lyrically, this is what I call a collision;
I'm on a mission,
Soaring high with eagle's vision.
And did I mention,
When I speak –
Jabbering Jaws drop,
The rotation of planet Earth seems to stops,
The whole world listens,
And there is always damage after the collision.

My poetry is;
Everyday reality –
Colliding into spirituality,
Rearranging lies into truth,
Restoring hope in lost youth,

I'm not a rapper – so don't compare me to those who are lost,
Great cost,
Has been paid,
For the words that I've laid –
From page-to-page.

The spoken words of poetry are like a volcano –
And it "ain't" no,
Other spiritual masterpiece,
That can release –
This kind of magnitude of human expression,
You've just collided into your first poetic lesson.

CHAPTER I
Interpretations

This chapter illustrates what I refer to as poetic revelations. It inspires prayer, influences the importance of meditation, and invokes intense thought. The deeper meaning of poems is often veiled within similes and metaphors. Although there are many ways to interpret one poem, the idea and/or message within epic poetry always expresses objectivity. This chapter captures a woven concept of philosophy, theology, psychology, and sociology. Each poem within this chapter possesses a poetic twist – a vague understanding for daily readers, and a deeper meaning for those who desire to research, meditate, and carefully consider each stanza.

The Forbidden Tree

Every time I hear the sound of a harp –
It kindles my memories of your soft gentle touch,
And I get a rush,
As the notes of a flute reminds me of how you –
Eat the things you do,
And add so much zeal into my existence.

And every night –
Your presence alone seems to chase away my blues,
Your soft silky touch comforts me –
And that's why I want to be,
Permanently –
Sealed in this season next to your body.

From my celestial crown,
Down –
To the souls of my useless feet –
Mentally, I've got you and spiritually you've got me.
For you are to me –
As a queen is to her king,
Symbolizing;
Your body is hypnotizing –
Pleasant royalties into my life,
For you've loved me more than paradise.

As the night,
Continue –
Down the jewel of my endless Nile,
I trust,
That lust,
Must –
Be your mind's most enticing thought.
Truly you ought –
To hear your heart pulsate;
From love to hate –
In rhythms of addiction.

Simply thinking of you causes my tender heart to flutter,
I've even convinced you that no other,

Has made my eyes whale up in tears –
When I faced the fear;
Of this season changing;
Time will soon be rearranging –
Into eternity,
And my desire,
Is that you experience the fire,
Of my destiny.
Your own heel would've surely bruised my head,
But instead –
You chose to stay,
For this reason
Some seasons –
Never seem to go away.

Fertile autumn,
Always reminding me,
Some kind of sign I see,
In the love you believe –
We share each day,
Hear me carefully when I say,
Deceitfully;
I'm sliding subtly through the earth,
Eating dust as it surfaces from the dirt,
Lying, on my belly and between each line -
I am cunningly trying,
To redefine humanity.
Behold; the forbidden tree,
Standing eastward within –
The Garden of Eden.

I'm seeing,
Fig leaves –
Falling off the branches of human trees,
That Adam never even knew existed.
I am the fruit, and carnal eyes can't resist this,
Lying in the mist of -
Fallen
Autumn
Painted
Leaves.

Poor Eve –
Wasn't intended to be a seamstress,
But Adam's helpmate became the serpent's mistress;
Oppressed and possessed,
Yet stressed by the reality,
That –
Lust turns nudity,
Into a kind of beauty –
That's never meant this much to me.
I'll send cold chills up your spine,
Put knowledge in your carnal mind –
Of good and evil,
I'm seeing feeble,
Slim,
Bare tree limbs –
Stretched-out waiting on the chill of winter.
I am that deep-dark-deceptive winter;
Springing-up in summer heat flashes.
For whatever it's worth,
I am fertilizing the earth.
As she anticipates,
The very thing her creator hates –
My melting snow,
And did you know –
There are night
Lights
In the sky,
That follows us wherever we go.

I'm drifting somewhere in between
Outer space and infinity,
I'm tasting melancholy drops of eternity,
Time is stalling;
The apocalypse is crawling,
Creeping –
In slow motion;
Autumn's leaves are falling;
The world is sinning,
And seeing –
The whole earth revolving -
Redundantly around the forbidden tree.

How Can You Resist This

Sitting and listening to a slow beat,
With an up tempo,
My thoughts –
Ought
To be labeled confidential,
Nothing in life is incidental –
I've discovered,
And uncovered;
Unveiled –
And prepared to tell –
The fact,
That –
The second reason I exist,
Is to resist –
Fruits of ignorance
Thoughts that make no sense,
I need no knowledge of sin;
Interruptions that only creep in –
My mind,
Trying to redefine –
My daily dose of destined reality,
I'm on a search for spiritual liberty –
Which is predestined for me.
The depths of my mentality –
Is where my exploration,
Begins,
And
Never ends.

I'm casting down wayward imaginations,
Erasing abbreviations:
Those not worth trying to understand,
I'm becoming more than mortal man;
A new creature,
With celestial features,
Like when a caterpillar becomes a butterfly,
There's no reason why,
With these wings I can't fly.

Stop daydreaming and wandering,
And start pondering:
Meditate –
That's what the devil hates.
Get preoccupied,
Inside –
Your mind.

The most confusing thing,
Seized in between –
Time and eternity,
Is humanity.
What is time –
Compared To eternity.
My flesh is only a temporal fabrication,
Through sequential contemplation;
If I think straight I can flee –
Beyond the borders of mortality,
And it is no coincidence,
Veracity is the evidence.
Every man has a soul,
Which can control –
His own reality.
Immortality,
Is trapped inside my mind,
Trying to find –
A way of escape.

The flesh hates –
To meditate,
Because the Word of God increases our faith.
When the human mind concentrates,
Reality vibrates,
All hell within the center of the Earth shakes,
The cycle of sin brakes,
My perseverance makes –
The thunder from heaven quake,
Then time takes –
My mind,
To another level –
Although I continue to find,

Myself existing,
Somewhere in between –
That confusing thing,
Called time and eternity;
The abyss.

Remember this –
Some things,
Aren't always the way they seem;
When you first learn,
That you've just been used or burned –
Time travels sluggishly,
But pleasant moments and memories,
Increase the subliminal velocity –
In the matrix of time.

Your mind –
Has the power
To turn an hour –
Into infinity
That's eternity;
Time without end,
But you chose to pretend –
And live within
This emotional whirlwind
Rather than
Digging in –
Your soul
And using thought to take control –
Of your situation.

Why are you wavering and hesitating,
Waiting anxiously, yet procrastinating.
Waiting to enter a world where time doesn't exist,
Pessimistically pondering in the abyss.
Choosing to stand in the mist –
Of poverty, pollution and perversion.

I've seen promises and blessings on an endless list –
Therefore, I do not understand, "How can you resist this?"

Peebles

She was unlike any woman I'd ever met,
She was so alluring and I'll never forget,
The way she redefined the definition of color:
Her smooth skin looked like honey-glazed butter.
She made the entire human race
Sisters and brothers –
Even turned out housewives and single mothers.
Rumor has it, that she goes both ways,
But this Saturday night I chose to play.

It was right
Before midnight
When I asked for her name,
But she was the author of another book called *Spitting Game*.
So she changed and rearranged the direction of my conversation,
Made all kinds of insinuations,
Seemed like she new all my problems,
Even had the solution as to how to solve them.

I should have known something had to be wrong –
When she insisted that I take her home.
The next morning my soul had been drained,
Her makeup was off and her face looked plain,
I was lying naked on the floor,
And my blinded eyes foolishly wanted more,
I still didn't even know her name,
She took me higher than that thing called "Mary Jane,"
But somehow she managed to move through my veins –
Controlling my brain,
Made me forget about my heartaches and pain.

When I opened my red-shot eyes she was gone,
I was alone –
In my empty
Soon to be,
Foreclosed home;
Female dog walked away with everything I'd ever owned.

She got me to a point where I'd do anything,

Even put a nine-millimeter to my own father's head,
And said –
"Give me those wedding rings!"
Hearing my mother scream –
As she dumped-out her purse,
I felt cursed.
But I refused to apologize,
Because my desperate mind had been hypnotized;
Under Peeble's spell,
Living in a crack-head's hell –
I wasn't a robber or a thief,
I was just desperate for another relief.
And something was very wrong,
The way she had me sucking on –
"Crystal glass sticks,"
Trying to get –
One quick fix,
My entire life turned into all of this,
Seemed like one night,
But that nameless game took half of my life.
And even though my mind has been set free,
Sometimes I still see –
Her walking in and out of church doors,
Scattered around on vacant apartment floors,
Robbing federal banks,
Shooting blank –
Hopes into desperate minds,
Misleading the blind;
She's that
Thin
Fine
Line –
Between love and hate,
She was my biggest mistake.

I cut her thoroughly with a razor blade,
But she still had me wearing shades,
At midnight,
Underneath the corner light,
Had me living the street life.

My winter-coat in the summer-heat eases the cold-chills of human-
hatred.
She broke my heart;
Had me trying to collect the pieces of my life in a stolen shopping-
cart.
Even in the winter sometimes I breakout in a cold sweat,
So it's difficult for me to forget –
The way people pass by me
Briskly,
And act as though I'm not standing there,
So I speak publicly to my make-believe friends –
And pretend
That someone cares.

She'll relax your mind,
If you give her the time
With the kind –
Of imitational love
That'll make you think her love is true,
But do you really think a pimp loves his prostitute -
Neither does his whore care about you.

Her weak-minded love slaves nicknamed her "CoCo"
But she's the kind of chef that poisons you to die slow
She'll kill you on the low-low
I later found out her name was Pebbles,
She was the first daughter of the devil,
Cooking with baking soda, metal spoons, and *cracked* pots
Freebasing with infested needles and tying tight knots
Looking for a visible vein
Never even asking your name
Simply sleeping and creeping,
From man to man –
Spreading like a disease,
And waiting to squeeze,
The hope out of your life.

Paris

Sitting here in my European riverboat,
Her love makes me float;
The Seine River is drifting me,
Paris is lifting me –
She is my "Place of Peace."
And I'm just waiting to release.

I'm painting Paris,
Gentle-wet French kisses I will always cherish,
I'm sculpturing the past,
So that our futures can last –
Forever.

The architect of Paris is so clever,
Uncertain if the Creator has ever
Designed another –
A town so fine;
"A town like a woman with flowers in her hair,"
Beauty so rare.

Why must my "Place of Peace" be so far,
I'm longing to hand-feed her caviar,
While sipping fine wines,
I'm tasting the elaborate design –
Of Paris.

I see –
Only you and me,
Staring,
Eye to eye, while wearing –
Nothing,
In the Palace de la Concorde.

I'm climbing snow-peaked-mountain tops,
I'm seeing clear melting water drop,
The temperature is tremendously hot,
And particularly,
I'm remarkably –
Impressed.

My riverboat;
Floats –
Through
Ile de la cite,
To Ile St. Louis,
I'm kneeling
I'm seeing nothing less
Than my celestial goddess.
The two of us isolated,
Eagerly we both anticipate it –
So I just keep on rowing.

Alexander;
Greek mythology –
Is what Paris is to me,
An ancient luxury,
A treasured mystery,
Hidden behind groves of silvery olive trees.
Celibate – and waiting on me,
A perfect sculpture of commitment and loyalty.

I'm running my hand through the wetness –
Of the Loire River,
She'll never forget this –
The way I made her shiver.

The most beautiful city in the world;
Eternally my girl.
I'm forever chasing –
Around that great river basin,
That flows out of Paris.

I'm dirty dancing in Paris,
Speaking French in sign language,
Painting hot springs in the deep-tranquil Seine River,
And sculpturing
The most dazzling
Cathedral dome,
I'm standing alone –
In the presence of a beautiful Obelisk from Egypt.

Sapphire Statue

I am a six-foot steep
Sapphire statue,
Standing in the abyss,
Senselessly wearing –
Nothing,
But a caramel glaze.

Beaten by southern sunrays,
Counting calendar days,
Inhaling the aroma of loneliness,
And she hasn't even noticed this –
Bleeding heart drained to complete emptiness.

Waiting patiently on a change,
Hoping that time will have mercy and rearrange –
My forsakenness,
Then clothe my nakedness.

She sculptured me touching myself;
With an empty ink pen,
In my *left* hand.
I am saying –
Nothing.

Painful experience;
When love won't love you back.
In fact,
I've lost track,
Of the exact –
Moment you left two sets of unexpected
Footprints trailing across my heart.

It's as if from the start,
You never expected what we had to last,
But you stayed and stole fragments of my past,
Turned my heart of flesh –
Into a sapphire stone which can only be caressed –
By you.
Please try to see through,

My teary eyes.

I'm a prisoner of desire,
And my prison walls are made of sapphire,
I'm oppressed,
By the love that once possessed,
My whole soul.

Take your chisel of love, come back and free me,
Don't make me daydream for eternity,
See these waterfalls running briskly –
Across sapphire,
I am constantly crying tears of passion,
And aching with desire.

The Third Eye

Scholars have attempted to study my philosophy.
Psychologist have evaluated,
Yet under-estimated
My mental capacity.

My carnal minded enemies,
Have tried to understand my theology,
But in addition to many years of college,
You must first recognize the power of street knowledge.

We all see things differently,
But the fact is –
There is
Only one true reality,
That's why
The third eye
Stolen from Egyptian philosophy
Now called Greek mythology
Was intended to be
The universal icon of intellectual unity.

Living without knowing the meaning of life,
Is like stabbing reality in the back with a knife.
I refuse to live then die,
Without aiming to understand of the reason why.

Life ought to be filled with purpose,
But so many awesome people
Failed to even notice –
Their intensified greatness,
So they settle for much less,
Thinking that life is just –
Some superficial test,
The best –
Is yet to come,
Stop and prepare your mind for the rest.

Because human existence can be confusing and diabolical,
But one who does not exercise the brain is intellectually suicidal,
So don't get caught up in the American cycle –
Your life is more meaningful than your professional title.

Do you control the brain or does it control you,
Why do people do the things they do,
And whichever answer you come up with,
Then explain to yourself what controls it.
These are questions that stimulate meditation,
Causing inner vibrations –
That provokes virtual concentration.
The third eye –
Can never lie,
It's synoptic;
Progressive like the future and even time cannot stop it.

The third eye is like a sixth sense,
It allows mankind to condense,
Unlimited information,
And build a supernatural relation –
Between purpose and power.

CHAPTER II
Faces of Reality

Life has a way of presenting situations and circumstances to us undesirably. Each epic poem in this chapter captures and illuminates harsh truths. My choice of words reflects the passion and reality of individuals who face such challenges on a daily basis. My poetry renders tribute to everyday individuals who manage to heroically triumph over and routinely face life's obstacles. I pray that my words accurately reflect our struggles and clearly illuminate the faces behind the words that often go unspoken.

Free Your Mind

I've done my research,
And I'm prepared to approach,
The roots of this sensitive topic,
And nothing on earth can stop it.

Because my thoughts have
Already collided into spoken words,
And for the sake of the entire nation –
I must be heard.

The subject of this lesson –
Is addressing,
Young black men,
Living –
In the heart of the *full circle*,
Exhausting your life jumping through hurdles.

You've taken your slave name,
Joined a violent gang,
And seem determined to remain –
A street thug,
Trying hard to become a prison *jitterbug*.

You're not unable,
Because you're capable,
You're just blind to the fact,
That your black mind is valuable,
So you refuse to use it.
Big faces on dollar bills –
Possess you to kill.

"Ain't" nothin' nice,
To a five or six point star,
Behind the bars
Of prison life.

Some pitchforks go up,
Others are pointed down,

All gangster kings don't wear imperial crowns,
Gangs colors don't matter six feet in the ground
And the knowledge of three hundred and sixty degrees,
Will never be broken down,
This is why gangs will always be around.

Because this distorted,
Unsorted
Sense of street loyalty,
Is a trend in urban society.

The new-age bastard child of teenage poverty,
It even limited my abilities,
Made me numb to human feelings,
At first I wasn't willing,
But like a thief in the night,
I knew it wasn't right,
But in order to get respect –
I started killing.

The mystery of this problem is like a riddle;
What do you call innocent victims
And single mothers who get caught up in the middle?
The twisted riddle goes something like this;
The stray bullet is shot by the fatherless,
While driving by you shoot aimless,
And then you miss,
And another weeping mother ends up childless,
And the death of her innocent child
Is totally meaningless.
Psychologically what do you call this?

When you listen to gangster rap
You better read between the lines,
Because while these stage-thugs are still entertaining
You'll be locked up doing time.
With their lyrics they're trying to amuse you,
But your male aggression
Has gotten caught up in the beat,
And once again they've confused you,
Now you're carrying heat,

And that's how I know –
Lyrically,
They've mentally
Abused you.

Put on your seatbelt and let's go for a ride,
Tightly close your eyes,
While I take your mind inside –
This thing called the urban matrix.

Chiraq, can you see yourself –
Walking around putting on a facade;
Iced out,
You know what I'm talking about;
Pants hanging,
Gold dangling,
Trying to act hard.
You need to get a job,
But instead you choose to rob,
Your own black brothers and sisters,
With drugs and prostitution.

Unfortunately, you're living under an illusion,
And your final conclusion,
Will be behind bobbed wired fences,
Because you've handcuffed your mind in false pretenses,
Of poorly thinking that your "thugged-out" erroneous fantasy,
Would lead you to a prosperous reality,
But you're sadly mistaken,
And you'll soon be awakened.
Philosophically – I'm hypnotizing you and taking,
Your carnal mind to another level.
This is an exorcist,
Emanuel has risen for me to do nothing less,
I rebuke the devil,
Now lower the treble,
While I increase the base,
And erase then replace,
The matrix.

Metaphorically, I'm like a brain surgeon,
Lyrically, I'm painstaking urging,
All young souls to listen.
The X-generation is missing,
The most important psychological dimension,
Of cerebral pretense.
We no longer value human life,
But we're drowning in technological intelligence.
Violent video games have contaminated brilliant brains.

Finally, I must mention,
That if you've been listening,
You're mind no longer has to be imprisoned.
Free your mind and the rest will follow,
Don't be color blind, and don't be so shallow.

Babies Having Babies

Her heart was just looking for somebody to love,
And only the past knows what her mind was thinking of.

Nine months of trial and tribulation
Ridicule and humiliation,
All these things she went through,
As ecstasy led her to,
A baby with a deadbeat for a father,
Who never even bothers
To pay attention,
Or even mention,
The child he helped to create,
And by the time the father becomes a man –
It'll be too late.

An abortion
Was out of the question,
Because that's not even her style,
Social workers suggested that she give up her child,
Like the Egyptian Pharaoh who forced Moses' mother
To place her child,
In the Egyptian Nile.

She thought she could handle anything,
Until she was placed with the responsibility of raising a black king –
In a jungle –
Called a ghetto.

She was struck with an infiltrating pain,
When she found out she was pregnant –
All because of the boyfriend game,
Now she needed to name –
The future.

Her step-father raised his hand and asked her –
"Who the hell do you think you are?"
She said he took things a little to far.
So she placed her son on her hip
While squinting her eyes she said, "Man, you a trip."

She stumped across the floor
Walked out and slammed the door –
At first she had to live in a shelter,
Until her welfare –
Kicked in
Then,
Things got somewhat better.

She adapted to the single-mother life,
And think she's making it just fine,
The alternative high school has a daycare –
So now she goes to school sometimes.
Every now and then she gets a little depressed,
Having a baby as a teenager isn't quite the life of success.
And while all of this –
Is going on,
Something is very wrong,
Because another teenage girl is "laying-up" with some small minded
boy;
Who thinks that having sex is like playing with a human toy,
"Use it,
Abuse it –
Then throw it away" –
Is what young brothers say,
While hanging-out shooting basketball on Saturday afternoons,

It is entirely to soon –
For you to use,
Your body to reproduce,
Although you have the physical capability,
You're mind is still not mentally
Ready –
To take care of,
And show the kind of love –
A child truly needs.

What makes you think you're any different from your deadbeat
father,
Who never even bothered –
To stick around,
To break life down.

It's a disaster,
To see young brothers reproducing bastards –
Right before the Master's –
Eyes.

Caught Up In The Cycle

I was born addicted to drugs,
My blood was afflicted
Because my pregnant mother used illegal drugs,
And my juvenile delinquent father was an absent thug.

This is how I entered my cycle of sin,
At the moment I was born
Seemed like my life came to an end.

Twice dead,
Is what the Newspapers read,
When the physician said
That
Drugs, gangs and violence brainwashed my head,
And although everybody has a story to tell,
My voice is echoing from the belly of hell.

I started off as a lil' shorty selling dope,
Because I wanted to make enough money,
To buy my poverty stricken family an ounce of hope.

Penny pitching in the streets I had to play the role,
So when times got rough I sold my burning soul,
I didn't even know
The value of life,
I was caught up in the cycle and didn't have time to think twice.

As if that wasn't enough,
I had to deal with more stuff,
I was faced with finding a quick and easy way to support,
The mistake that my teenage *baby-Momma* refused to abort.

Now I am the locked up absent father,
I want to change my ways,
But sometimes I ask myself, "Why even bother?"
Because it seems like there's no way to redirect my cycle;
Unfortunately,
I'm like all
The ghetto-stricken generations that came before me,

Even though this is not what I want to be,
So now I'm trying to make a deal with destiny,
But even he keeps telling me,
Nothing in life is free.

It's evident that I'm living a curse –
But what worse,
Is my inability to break this cycle of sin,
That keeps destroying –
My hopes and dreams,
I feel like a dethroned king;
My life seemingly doesn't mean a thing.
For the first time in my life I feel a real need,
To drop down to my knees,
And cry out
Mercy please,
Freeze
Time,
Before it squeezes
The hope out of this life of mine.

My soul is desperately trying,
My spirit is slowly dying,
But hopelessly I keep buying -
my own lame excuses.

Now I understand,
That I need to stop playing,
Because it's time for me to stand,
On my own to two feet,
And beat –
This cycle of sin.

Dear D.A.D.,

I cannot stand the fact,
That –
The blood of an unknown man rushes through my veins.
The thought of a stranger's infidelity is driving my brain insane.
I often wondered if I knew you, would my life be drastically different,
Or would things simply remain the same.

You must be my worse curse.
Daily living inside of me,
An internal reflection of what I cannot see.
Intimate knowledge revolving,
Voices from the abyss calling,
Out my name,
Like a guessing game,
With no answer.
I'd rather be dying of cancer,
Than to be your son,
I'd already lost before my natural life begun.

Just like crapping-out on a pair of black dice,
Gambling with life.
You won an embryo,
But decided not to watch it grow.
If it weren't you, than it certainly would have been a better man,
Somebody to break life down,
Or just be around,
Or even hold,
My cold
Hand.

Should I hate you for what you didn't do,
Or despise you for the tribulation you put my mother through.
As far as I'm concerned you died when I was born,
And any possible father to son relationship has been torn –
It's obvious that you didn't respect it,
Because you disappeared and rejected it.

What were you thinking of -
You should have appreciated my mother's love,

But you procrastinated,
Waited and waited,
Now it's to late for it,
And you're almost hated –
By the greatest child you biologically created.

My invisible Papa,
Where were you –
When I was being beat by my stepfather,
You didn't even bother
To pick up a telephone and call,
In fact, you did nothing at all.
Now what's the lame excuse –
You're going to use.
I'm sure you had a telephone,
My invisible Papa - the rollin' stone,
Wherever you laid
With an unpaid
Woman,
And started cumin' –
You called your home.

Haven't you seen the commercials on child support.
And why would you try to convince my mother to abort,
And kill,
Against her will,
Your own child living in her womb,
But then again I guess you left too soon,
To lay your filthy hand on her swollen stomach –
In order feel my tender heartbeat,
You were too eager to run off and cheat.

At least that's what I was told
And now that I'm old
I've heard the other side
Glad you never died
When my anger suffocated you with words
Based on the lies I'd heard

These are the unspoken word I was forbidden to repeat,
Rejection and neglect travels deep

You treated my mother like she was cheap
You deserved to be called a creep
Since my southern mother was other woman –
And the northern woman was really your wife.
Yeah, later on in my mother's life,
Without a doubt,
She found out,
I know a few things I'm talking about.

I've thought about your deceptive ways,
For years I counted calendar days –
Waiting your return...
It wasn't until later that I learned,
The meaning of a deadbeat dad,
Accepted the absence of what other kids had –
Somewhat sad;
The pain you inflicted,
The child you resisted.
But then again,
When my mother and father forsake me – the Lord shall take me in.

My mother is one of sensitivity,
Who taught me to avoid negativity.
Which is the perfect explanation,
Why there was always a hesitation –
When I asked about the father I'd never known.
For years I thought it was something I'd done wrong –

So my mother chose not to speak of you,
She too,
Tried desperately,
But unsuccessfully –
To bury you.
These aren't just words filled with hate,
I can relate.
Although your biggest mistake –
I forgive,
Because I don't want to live,
With the vile thought of you behind the veil of my imagination,
So you will always be thought of as an *unexplained abbreviation*;
A meaningless acronym,

An old slave hymn:
Thoughts –
That ought not exist.
I am a bastard child,
Although it has taken a long while
For me to excel –
Righteousness always prevails.

I am digging a six-foot whole in the ground,
Without even looking down –
I'm burying hopes and dream.
I'm a fatherless Prince becoming an African King.
Forsaken by the father who never wanted me,
But when my natural father forsook me,
My heavenly Father took me,
And somehow crowned me with deity –
Dignity and spirituality.

p.s. D.A.D., R.I.P.

Chocolate Child

Tell me what I should do when my parents don't teach me,
And the preacher can't reach me
And the streets become my home?
Where do I run when the police start to chase me,
And I think that I've done no wrong?

Sometimes it seems like the whole world is against me,
And I don't know where to turn,
So I turn to the streets and I run with my gang,
And this is how I learn.
So many people seem to disagree,
But your opinions have never helped,
And poverty only breeds grief.

Continuously
People ask me,
When I grow up what do I want to be.
But I don't even know what I currently need,
My soul is crying out for help,
And society
Is just watching me,
Slowly bleed.

My teacher's favorite question is,
"Do you think you'll ever change?"
However politics has permanently arranged it –
So that poverty will stay the same.
With the unfortunate living in projects;
Small jungles made for broken-black-families –
Neighborhoods designed,
With x-convicts in mind,
No hope for black men,
So we try to survive however we can.

When I open my "frig" to find something to eat,
Emptiness seems to take me to another realm of defeat.
Everywhere I look a cockroach seems to crawl,
And stray bullets from the neighborhood –
Have gotten many whole in our walls.

Daily I fight this war
These are the battles of the poor,
Life persuaded me long ago,
That these things shouldn't be so,
Therefore, any opportunity I get, out the ghetto is where I plan to go.

They say I'm trapped in this world of confusion,
And illusions –
Of wealth and fame has gotten me defeated,
All because I'm a black man, it's obvious that I've been cheated.
That's why I found myself protection in knives,
And started taking lives,
With illegal guns,
And while the world is ignoring my problems,
My stray bullets are killing their teenage sons.

Some so-called brothers and sisters ended up just fine,
But they think they're too good for the others,
So they don't even waste their time.
They think that I'm not trying,
So they said that they're not buying –
My lame excuses.

But what they don't realize,
Is that I must wear this "thugged-out" disguise,
Because in the jungle I live in you must wear a hard shell,
Or folks in the hood will be able to tell –
That I laugh, I cry, and I talk,
In fact, I'm just like you, but you've been loved and handled with care,
And like an ugly stray-orphan I've been rejected and this is not fair.

So I dare,
You come here,
Acting like you care,
And judging my lifestyle –
Stick around for a little while,
And I bet you'll walk away crying,
When you see young souls dying,
Because we've decided to supplement illegal dope –
So that we can cope,
With our destitution and lack of hope.

Now I face another day,
With no hope of anyone to show me the way,
And as so-called black men march up and down my street,
They protest against the weapons that defend me.
What can anybody do...
To replace or erase,
The fact that,
Somewhere I have a father that I've never even known,
Take a picture of me,
Behind these prison walls –
So that he can see,
Just how far I've gone wrong.

And where is my hopeless mother that didn't want me selling drugs,
Has she forsaken her hopeless child and now considers him a thug.
They've given up on me,
And sometimes I see –
WHY.

By the streets I live,
And by the street I just might die.
I'm that chocolate child you failed to embrace,
Nothing seems to erase –
The neglect,
The disrespect,
The way people would reject –
My unattractive ways.
I'm the seed of a slave –
That lived years ago,
And now I've been born with his scar in my soul.
Wake up my people can't you see who I am,
The descendant of a nation – bound to be damned.

From Anger To Rage

The Oklahoma bombing,
Was inevitably coming
To pass.
America cultivated
And later hated
Her own mass,
Murderer.

Hear me when I say,
I watched and even wrestled –
With Timothy McViegh,
In his greatest rage,
As he carelessly set the stage,
To kill
Against the will –
Of God.

His anger got so agitated,
That on April 19, 1995 he assassinated,
168 innocent victims in the society he hated;
Even defenseless ladies –
And newborn babies.

Six years later,
American terrorism grew greater,
As Osama Bin Laden
Was assumed guilty for plotting –
The destruction
And distinction
Of the American way.

Fear caused America to kneel and pray,
Until September 11, became just another day,
Now Rage has possessed the Land of the Free –
To fight a spiritual war of principality,
We seek to destroy what which we cannot see,
And we –
Hide behind the statue of liberty,
Yet, we "hunt down to kill,"

And do whatever we feel –
In name of revenge.

When anger turns into a raging fire,
The human mind embraces only one desire,
And that –
Is pay-back,
Unmanaged anger will make you viciously attack.
"Revenge is mine," said the Lord,
So put down your weapons and pick up your Sword.
Before rage takes control,
Of your angry soul,
And it's very cold,
The way it will –
Make a confused child kill
His own brother,
Then make a young father disrespect his child's mother.
Like Cain killed Able,
These are all unstable –
Decisions,
Uncontrolled anger is like a satanic religion –
From hell,
And you can always tell,
When it's raging.

Many victims of rage are trapped within mental prisons,
Because they refused to listen –
To sound advice,
Refused to think twice,
And allowed rage to command their life.

Anger can be a positive force,
But of course,
We have to practice self-control,
Acknowledge the facts
And learn how to react
In order to stay – Focused.
The deep-felt passion that lives within raging souls,
Only develops and grows,
Within certain kinds,
Of human minds;

Those who know how to forgive,
Will live –
In harmony and peace.

There will always be
The influence of negativity;
Consistently trying
To get your deep mind,
To degenerate,
And deteriorate –
From anger into a negative rage.

Rage is walking around seeking a name and a face,
Trying desperately to erase and replace,
Your positive reputation;
Filling your head with insinuations,
Causing your blood to bubble,
Getting your flesh in trouble.
Rage will,
Cause a stray bullet to kill –
An innocent child,
Rage has its own style –
It doesn't care about you,
Or the things you do.

If you'd only release those dried up tears,
Your temper will slowly disappear,
Don't quickly embrace the fear
Of not protecting your emotions,
You're caught-up in the commotion –
Of anger,
And the danger,
Is that it's leading you to a world of rage.

A world that's very small,
Where feelings like love and mercy
Mean nothing at all.
Where you,
Only see through,
Reflections of blood-shot-red eyes,
You become hypnotized,

You no longer think,
Your love for life shrinks,
So you will even murder and kill,
Or do whatever you feel –
To get revenge.

My greatest enemy,
Is the rage inside of me,
The flaming fire that ignites –
And delights,
In anger.

The greatest danger,
Is that my soul becomes like a complete stranger:
Because when I'm upset,
My blank mind forgets,
And importance of everything,
Nothing seems to mean a thing.

Rage plays no guessing games,
Takes no prisoners, no names,
And claims –
To be,
The enemy,
Of reason.

But I'm still pleading to get you to understand,
That anger flows through my veins just like the next man,
But you can restrain the rage,
Before it engage,
Into something you'll regret,
Because most people will never forget,
The hurt and pain you've initiated.
All because you become agitated,
Your life turns to the page –
Entitled "From Anger to Rage."

The Love Of Money

America revolves around an axle of dead presidents,
And this is no coincidence.
Therefore I'm prepared to tell,
As my unfavorable lyrics unveil –
The evidence.

Sarcastically speaking it's incredibly funny,
How the love of money –
Can turn a drug dealer,
Into a serial killer,
Because you distribute lethal injections,
That cause temporary mental erections,
You carelessly sell,
Hells'
Merchandise,
Without even thinking twice.
Just like snake eyes on a pair of black dice,
The love of money has got you gambling
With your precious life.

If you click twice –
On rewind,
I'll virtually illustrate,
How it only took two steps,
For me to enter your one track mind;
The left foot is where I began,
The second step was only to get my right foot in;
I've seen your whole world rotating around green papers.
You will kill,
For a bill,
You've become a disgrace,
To our black race,
The way you chase -
After dead Presidents,
And it's no coincidence –
The way you race,
Behind lifeless white men,
As fast as your black end can.
They've manipulated you into carry a gun,

Set you free only within the boarders of the ghetto –
And said run – "nigger" run.

Big faces,
Never replaces –
A prostitutes' human dignity,
For a few minutes of ecstasy,
She'll sale herself for a twenty spot –
And this is the naked truth whether you like it or not.
Some whores do it,
Because they're really into it,
Others do it to stay alive and survive.
If hating me helps her change her ways and feel better,
Than let her -
Hate me for what I have to say,
Personal feelings oftentimes stand in the way,
Of black beautiful queens –
With very low
And sometimes no – self esteem.

You'll soon see,
That the love of money –
Is unequivocally,
The root of all evil,
Your greedy-unthankful flesh,
Has made your hungry mind
Intellectually feeble.
So you can't comprehend –
That you're living in
One big casino,
And you're loosing fast,
But you don't know,
How to stop,
So quitting is not –
An option.

Your love of money is an addiction,
You need it like AIDS infected crack heads need nutrition,
Making big money seems to be your only ambition.
And did I mention –

Your philosophy,
Is not that hot to me,
Because mentally you're still broke,
Your entire life is one big joke.

You're hustling for nickels and dimes,
It's ironic how you're trying,
To make more and more money,
But you're wasting your time.
And the very thing you've wasted,
Nothing can replace it,
Time moves forward –
And all the money in the world cannot retrace it.

This was the ending,
But I'll speak slower and start from the beginning –
The love of money is the root of all evil.

The Revolution - WWIII

Now that God has changed my street ways,
Took the profanity out of what I have to say;
The mass majority
Of this upper class society,
Expects me to become their black converted hero;
They say, "Have pity, and
Mentor in the inner-city."

But I will not allow my generation to feel cheated,
By the conceited –
Views of popular belief,
I am not a thief –
Nor a prostitute,
I am a product of the institute –
Of "Hard Knox."

So your worldviews will not pimp me,
Over one hundred years ago,
Black beautiful slaves fought to be free,
And one of those slaves represented me.
And now you don't want me to say "nigga,"
Because I demanded you not to say it,
You don't want me to play pro sports,
Because I play them better than you play it.
And when I speak Ebonics, you say I'm politically incorrect,
So you give me no respect,
And you wonder how "I dance under waterfalls and not get wet."

Don't you know I'm the product of a new nation,
The millennium child of the x-generation,
My culture is born through the vibes of every Christian radio station.

Call no man a Fool,
Don't you know how cool –
I am
And whether you like me or not,
I don't give a –
Uncle Sam
Does not control my destiny,

I've spoken –
Behold: A blessing, I've broken –
The curse and declared my own liberty.

While you're secretly hiding and praying
The devil is constantly and actively saying,
"I'm more than just the attitude of hip-hop,
I'm the force behind a nation that armies cannot stop.
I have no race – I transcend like that,
I have no creed – I descend like that,
I trust no man – but some people think I just pretend like that.

Every teenager will soon be under my spell,
And every young adult will soon wear my hard shell,
Because in this kingdom I'm building you've got to 'ride or die,'
I've established new laws – it's called 'an eye for an eye.'
Who needs your laws and old school traditions?
All eyes are on me –
In this backward society,
Nobody listens –
They only petition,
Against the next man,
Even though they don't understand –
The daily struggle behind the influence of sin."

Since you'll listen as I speak their *unspoken words*,
This is the street testimony I heard:

"When I'm riding around beating my beats,
I've got to carry my heat,
'Wootay,' you know I'm living the thug life:
No time and no mind to think twice.
Statistically, I'm just another –
Confused brother,
Trapped inside the game,
Trying to maintain,
Seeking material gain,
Conquering financial strain,
Overcoming emotional pain,
Dodging pale fingers as they point the blame,
And living life with a stolen slave name."

Take notes –
Of the *unspoken word* trapped within quotes.

Metaphorically, Ebonics describe America as being "hot,"
Culturally we're considered a melting pot,
And while black activist are fighting for racial integration,
This country is still infected with continued segregation.

So the devil has decided –
And tried it,
He said, "This world is my own.
I'll treat humans like puppets –
And make sure no one gets alone."
Trust no man,
Is what he's saying,
And only stand –
Up
For what you believe,
Let no man deceive
You into converting,
He's alerting,
The hip-hop nation,
The x-generation,
Your teenage child,
And after a while;
Behold,
Satan is powerless
Unless
He uses your seed,
To feed –
The world,
Every man, woman, boy and girl.

The only way to conquer the past,
And make sure the curse doesn't last –
Is to forgive it,
And not relive it.

It's no secret that the pale-faced Anglo Saxon man,
Strategically planned,

Drugs in the ghetto and –
Black on black crime,
BUT now it is time,
To turn the page,
And set the stage,
For a spiritual revolution.

I know it's funny how the Constitution,
Declares the institution
Of the freedom of speech.
I've heard and seen the things white racist teach,
What's even worse is the messages black hypocrites preach.
They've used the constitution to say, "Your lifestyle,
Is not worthwhile.

But soon they will see,
There will no longer be –
Any need for college.
God will give you the authority,
To rule the world lyrically –
With *prophetic street knowledge*;
Morally the whole world is bankrupt,
And from the core it will soon corrupt.

So right now I'm causing a revolution,
ONE by ONE,
I'm going to rid young people of the stuff called pollution.

Put your hands together, because I'm introducing –
A separation;
Holy sanctification.
I'm unveiling a new kind of segregation:
I'm separating light from night,
Wrong from right –
And the language the devil speaks will be like biblical Babel,
Even unto this very generation.
There's power in the blood,
Just like God I'm causing a flood,
And this time it won't be a simply interruption,
I'm talking brimstone, fire, and total destruction.

In the thug life,
You become filled with strife –
And anger
Like a nuclear time bomb – so they've labeled you DANGER;
Endangered species –
Is exactly what they said,
So before you're twenty-five they expect you to be dead.

But Maya Angelo,
You've reached my soul,
They don't know,
God's people still rise,
In every creed, culture and race,
Upon eagle's wings I'm setting the pace,
Onward Christian soldier,
I thought I told you.

I have no pity,
For no city,
Even though it may be falling,
Christ's name I just keep calling;
His name is a strong tower,
And His Spirit will soon shower –
On every man
AND
Every woman.

I've already initiated the revolution,
And World War III will not be over
Until Christ rides in with a final solution.

The Sound Of A Closing Prison Cell

Cling-Cling went the sound,
As my world came tumbling down.
The sound of a closing prison cell,
Is the closet thing to a living hell.

Graphic midnight sex and rape scenes,
AIDS infected Drug fiends,
Deadly violent gang scenes,
And other inhumane things –
I couldn't tell you if I tried,
But a part of my soul died;
Was it my pride,
Or my integrity,
Or my ability –
To become a productive part of this segregated society.

Cling-Cling went the sound
As my world came tumbling down.
The sound of a closing prison cell,
Is the closet thing to a living hell.
I've seen grown men use dried-up
Kool-aid and Ketchup
For make-up –
And called it
Lip stick.

Many nights I rushed into the latrine,
And stumbled upon a scene,
Of a masculine man sucking another man's –
Dick.

I've seen gangsters and thugs
Come in
As men,
And leave as whores and –
"Tricks."

Cling-Cling went the sound,
As my world came tumbling down.

The sound of a closing prison cell,
Is the closet thing to a living hell.

What is a prison guard to do,
When he walks into a filthy cell and only sees you,
With your naked body strapped into a wide-open position;
Legs stretched-out into a "Y" like dimension,
Chest-down on the table,
Bruised and battered body physically unable –
To move.

Tears fiercely falling,
From your black and blue eyes,
Rats aggressively crawling,
Toward your bloody thighs,
Because your blood is still dripping and streaming,
And in order to muffle your moaning and screaming;
Stuffed into your mouth was as a pair of semen –
Drenched prison issued underwear.

Question number one – does the guard even care.
And even if he cares about you,
There's only one thing that guard can do –
Announce an emergency code blue;
Attica's old call for medical attention,
And did I mention –
Cling-Cling went the sound,
As my world came tumbling down.
The sound of a closing prison cell,
Is the closet thing to a living hell.

Prison initiation introduced me to a new kind of segregation;
Where racism is convoluted, deeply rooted, polluted
And now instituted politically.
Coincidently,
Prison has cultivated its own society.
A place you can only pay attention
To true religion –
In the valley of your imagination,
A place where you never really sleep

Deep –
Unless you're locked alone isolation;
Even in segregation,
You better watch your back –
Because the guards have the keys and don't think they won't attack.

One dark night in prison
Will turn your world upside-down,
And if you pay attention
The unspoken word will resurrect your soul and turn your life around.

Prison is a place where your right-hand,
Will intimately become your best friend,
Where you'll speak out loud to your own inner-man.

The only thing you can truly do,
Is hope to heaven from your place of hell
Those sex predators and prisons pimps
Won't be able to tell –
The real you:
You're just a simple kid
From the hood,
Who got caught-up and did,
Whatever you could –
To fit in,
But then again,
Now that you've gotten caught up in the cycle,
You're like all –
The other brothers who surround you,
And you too,
Can only see through –
Prison bars and bobbed wired fences,
Because your carnal eyes were blind,
And your afflicted mind –
Was trapped in false pretenses.
So you're forced to wear that "thugged-out" shell,
Hoping that other prisoners won't be able to tell –
That you're trying to hide –
Your soft-gentle side,
But what you haven't recognized
Is the difference between,

Those two confusing things,
Called prison life and street life.

They are not the same,
You're playing a completely different game:
Where numbers represent your name,
Where nothing chasing away the pain,
Where no one accepts the guilt or blame.

Found myself trapped within a world of hate
Because I thought I could take,
Colds up my bosom and not be burned,
And I still haven't learned.

My biggest mistake,
Was that I waited too late.
Now I live life with a prison cellmate.

Cling-Cling went the sound,
As my world came tumbling down,
The sound of a closing prison cell,
Is the closest thing to a living hell.

Scared Sealed Lips

I'm about to reveal,
What my lonely heart has concealed –
All of my life,
My personal testimony of how the wrong outweighed the right.

My deepest hidden secret,
I've decided to no longer keep it,
I'm going to use my bitter history,
To make other people see –
Through
My strong-hard facade;
The adhesive protecting the shattered pieces –
Of my broken heart.

During my childhood I was physically abused.
The man who was suppose to love me used,
Lethal weapons to redirect my behavior,
My tear-dropped-filled pillow was my only savior.

My bruises have healed,
The scabs have peeled,
But a part of me has been scared forever,
And emotionally I don't know if my wounds will ever –
Heal;
And most people will never feel.
This kind of internal pain,
The way he would hit me, curse at me, and call me out my name,
I was played like a black-pawn in a bad chest game.
I had nothing to lose and nothing to gain.

For so many years,
I harbored so many fears.
I desperately wanted someone to rescue me,
But unfortunately,
I was too afraid to tell,
My scared sealed lips trapped me in the kind of hell,
Especially designed –
With certain kids in mind.

I wanted so bad,
To take the few-little things I had,
And just run-away,
But my mother's silent-love kept making me stay.

Deep within;
I guess I was expecting -
Something to magically change,
I thought maybe time would rearrange –
My daily routine.
But it seemed –
The better I behaved,
The more I was enslaved –
By his abusing ways.

And what I really hated,
Was the fact we weren't related,
But that did not negate it,
My comatose mind was sedated –
Because my human rights had been infiltrated
And violated.

I often wondered was it right;
Because he comforted my mother at midnight,
And caused me grief and pain,
Seemed to love my siblings and yet called me out of my name.
Some things I cannot explain.
Such as;
How do you point a loaded gun,
Into the face of your own stepson.
How do you push a defenseless child down a flight of stairs,
Then tell me –
How do you psychologically make a young boy feel like no one cares.

There was nothing I could do about it,
My dying spirit couldn't live with it,
But mentally,
Life began to mean so little to me –
That psychologically –
I couldn't manage to live without it.

Looking back in retrospect,
Trying to recollect,
Those things I'd forced myself to forget,
Desperately I tried
To hide
My tears on the inside,
But slowly they fell from my eyes,
Because the image of his evil face,
Was a close-up color caption I could not erase.

It was my stepfather,
And my sweet mother never bothered –
To complain,
So silently I endured the pain.
And it's really strange –
How he seems to have forgotten about all the abuse,
That was used.

Yet, I remember senselessly –
Balling up in the fetal position defenselessly;
I still have nightmares from what he did to me,
All because I was too afraid to tell,
I didn't see the purpose of going from one kind of hell,
To another one called a foster home,
So I built a giant-iron wall,
To protect my small –
Heart.
Closed myself in,
And called it home.
Surrounded by so many people,
But I'd become convinced that I was all alone –
Trying to survive,
This is just another reason why –
My healing-heart
Will always give thanks to the only God,
Because He never told my deepest secret –
No one else would have been able to keep it.

As you can see,
This is an epic poem about me.
Some situations you can simply change,

In other circumstances you must endure the pain.
But always remember the most empowering lesson you'll ever learn,
Life will take you through many turns;
And as strange as these words may sound,
When someone tears your spirit down,
Always forgive,
For this will empower the life you live.

My Mother's Nature

The seed was planted,
And my mother's nature granted
It the right to grow,
She didn't even know
What to expect,
Because time wouldn't allow her to futuristically reflect,
On invisible images,
But her love had no blemishes,
So she decided,
To try it.

She had the courage,
To bravely nourish,
Four tiny seeds –
Into sprouting trees,
Blooming flowers out of dying weeds,
She protected the honeycomb from the killer bees.

The honeycomb
Was my mother's fertilized womb,
And I was that dying weed,
But –
Bud first she set me free,
And just like that sprouting tree,
My roots go deep – from eternity to eternity.

My mother's nature;
Is the reason –
For the season of my earthly existence,
Her persistence –
Produced my eminence,
And my existence,
Is no coincidence.

Empirically I can relate,
To those they call bastards and mistakes,
But I will not allow fatherless anger and hate
To overtake
The great

Choice my mother chose to make.

She must be
Some kind of sparkle of divinity,
I was conceived inside of her,
But now she lives inside of me.
Sounds of sweet a melodies and harmony;
Her tender voice as she spoke to me,
While I was being nurtured inside of her body;
The safest place I've ever been,
Was when
I was hidden,
Inside my mother's womb.
Nine months was entirely too soon,
But destiny,
Had a plan for me.

She had vision for my life when I could not see,
So my mother painfully –
Pushed me into reality,
And I will always tenderly embrace,
The mother, whom even death cannot replace –
For this miracle God has produced,
And loosed –
Through her womb.

CHAPTER III
Eight Shades of Brown

As a Christian African American male author, I am honored to possess the privileged and opportunity to write a chapter of poetry, which commemorates the heritage of my own legacy. Each poem in this chapter identifies with views and opinions, which are not necessarily my own. Nevertheless, these views and opinions possess an extreme since of worth within the black community. So often, the black community is poorly represented; our social issues are ignored; the events of our history are seldom portrayed; and bitterness, reverse-racism, and anger have muffled the voice of our legacy. The eight poems in this chapter have rekindled that voice. These poems are the voice giving life to the experiences of our past. Each poem speaks the unspoken words of black people's emotions, attitudes, thoughts and dreams.

Black History

I leave behind me a legacy,
Of individuality –
Others will desire to be like me.

Because I'm that deep dark reality,
That lies far beneath what the naked eye can see.

This sacred-black veil,
Is the strong-dark shell,
That cannot be duplicated,
Even Einstein's –
Great mind,
Could not imitate it –
That's why others races hate it.

In the beginning darkness was upon the face of the deep,
Until God began to speak –
Then light began to creep.
Before there was light on earth,
There was night on earth,
The dark ages has declared my valuable worth.

I'm some kind of –
Reminder
Of how eternity is hidden inside of humanity,
Although white society,
Failed to see,
Because my colored caramel darkness limited their ability.

We were once numbered amongst the great majority,
Until our ancestors were stripped from their royal authority,
But when my enemies –
Saw there was no end to me,
They became intimidated,
Freed my flesh, but my black soul they still hated.
So they always attempt to relate it –
To something cursed,
Or even worse –
The word black,

Has been intellectually attacked.

Because we would not bow down to the portrait of a blue-eyed
Savior,
Their psychiatric analytical perspectives –
Could not dictate our behavior.

Webster could not define me,
So intellectually he tried to blind me,
With iron chains they tried to bind me –
They keep trying me,
Made an attempt of deceiving,
My kind into believing,
That our human worth was less than –
Even said that if you had a tenth of our blood
You were not a whole man.
They even painted make believe images,
On European canvases –
Of African dances;
Insulting sculptures of bare-feet women –
Performing,
Rituals in the nude.
Even their art intrudes –
Upon our history,
Polluting it with his story.

They,
Needless to say whom,
Because everybody understands,
That only the blue-eyed white man –
Beat our people down to their knees,
Roped their necks –
And left them dangling in southern trees.
Like strange fruit,
Sagging lifeless from the root –
Of racial hatred –
And segregated.
When a black man or woman died,
They –
Labeled our people N.H.I.:
No humans involved.

Raped our African maidens and called them belly warmers,
Chained our ancestors beneath the upper decks of enormous –
Slave ships,
Took long brutal trips –
Beat our people with leather whips,
Sold us on auction blocks,
Like live stock –
And called it slavery.

THESE
Unforgettable memories,
Will always be a part of me,
But ironically –
I'm the child of tranquility,
The father of victory,
And mentally –
I've triumphed over slavery.

But one short century,
Is far too soon to forget what they've done to me,
Yes, I said me,
Because they've tampered with my history,
With his story of cruel brutality –
They redirected my reality –
Literally.

And now they sit around acting as though,
They don't even know –
That slavery and sharecropping affected black people
Only one hundred years ago.
My grandparents hand-plowed the soil,
For this new world,
And you know they were treated brutally while enslaved;
Toiled from the rising of the sun,
To the going down of the same –
And never paid.
So don't sit there wondering why I'm outraged.

Now I want my forty acres and a mule
So they think I'm just an African acting a fool,

But as long as we keep playing it cool,
They
Refuse -
To pay attention to you,
But I can see straight through –
Their cunning façade,
It's not very hard.

Now maybe you'll comprehend,
Why many blacks don't trust pale-faced men,
The reason many of my people despise white skin,
This is no excuse, simply that you might understand –
Bruised hearts cannot pretend.

For you,
I know it's very scary,
For me to say –
By any means necessary.
I'm not a racist,
But I cannot erase this,
I try diligently not to be prejudice,
Because I'd rather spend my dying time,
Trying –
To solve this cruel confusing puzzle called life.

This is simply a black man's point of view,
But most people will never be able to see through –
Their angry eyes,
And this is no surprise,
Because even some colored folks have been hypnotized –
Into believing the white man's historical lies.

I have a name,
That whips and chains cannot replace,
I come from a place,
That slavery cannot erase.

I am more than the complexion of dark skin,
Some caramel colored people are trapped within –
Chains of black discrimination,
Therefore,

Before I can bond with the pale-faced man,
I've got to free the black mind from self-hatred
And self-segregation,
Therefore my lips are calling on the participation –
Of black society.

Quietly.

I'm about to change reality,
Like the author and director Spike Lee,
I'm rewriting and directing my own destiny,
And the final chapter will be –
Futuristically;
A world that revolves around
Colored caramel kings and queens –
Who look just like me.

dreaming of africa

i breathlessly gazed
with an amazed
look in my eyes
wondering how wise
must they have been
to build
beautiful ancient egyptian
pyramids that touch the peak of the blue sky
the truth cannot lie
i've tasted the salty waters of the atlantic
although i couldn't stand it
i've traveled, shackled, and chained from the ivory coast
to the world's worst
nation in the universe
from botswana to zambia
from zaire to nigeria
i've never been inferior
to another man
i've never been intimidated by discolored pale skin
africa is the place where my spirit will always be
i can still hear the tribal beats of victory
echoing from ethiopia
although i've never told you
my soul is standing along the atlantic coast
watching the most
beautiful sunrise
the manifestation of a miracle
captured within the reflection of my dark brown eyes

The Brotherhood

Segregated worlds colliding,
And people are hiding –
Their true colors,
Just because you're black on the outside
Doesn't mean that you're my brother.

My brother can be,
Unequivocally,
Intellectually –
Compared to me,
Mentally,
He'll control who and what he wants to be,
I am eternally
A part of the brotherhood of liberty.

It's more to the struggle of life,
Than racial discrimination between blacks and whites.
Seems like we fight –
Day and night
In this power struggle of interracial tug of war,
And the harder we pull,
The rich keep getting richer,
And the poor keep getting poorer.

My thoughts
Ought –
To be labeled confidential,
Because I publish unspoken words that are essential,
To reality, liberty and spirituality.
When I exhale,
My ever-running mind expels –
Exact
Facts.

Sinners will not like it,
Because they'd rather believe in psychics,
But I have the spiritual IQ of a prophetic genius,
And I mean this –
When I say

I pray
That my words will reveal,
The truth, which has been concealed,
About black history,
Human ability,
And true spirituality.

Why should I trust you,
When I can see through –
Your hypocritical disposition,
You look directly into my eyes when I speak,
And in responding your lying-lips prove that you've failed to listen.

Everyday I live within,
This multicultural world wind,
And I make heads spin,
When –
I unveil the mystery,
That we live in a society,
Where I cannot make my blackness my first priority.

In fact, my nationality,
Is officially,
And invisible entity –
Of virtual reality.
I'm simply a mind invoking force,
Taking carnal minds on an unending course.

Therefore,
Your –
Afro-centric complexion,
Doesn't mean a thing to me.
I'm more so interested in the liberty –
Of mankind's mentality.

But unfortunately,
It's sadly amusing,
That my black brothers keep confusing,
Brotherhood with blackness –
When most blacks are doing prison time,
Not for inter-racial relations –

But black on black crime,
You must be out of your mind;
Bamboozled,
Had,
Hoodwinked,
Meaning that your eyes must have blinked –
In the ghetto, if you even think –
That I equate brotherhood to the color of brown skin.
Think again;
Cain relentlessly killed his brother Able,
Judas betrayed Christ after sitting at the same table,
A true brotherhood must be tested and stable.

It's imperative for you to understand,
That according to African
American
History,
Which is an unavoidable reality,
The chocolate covered man,
Will sometimes stab you in the back quicker than –
The Anglo Saxon.

I'm the brother of the Black Panther,
Who was bit by a dog,
Hosed down by a P.I.G.,
And carried away on a horse.
And ironically,
You just happen to be,
The enemy of the widow;
Who lost her Mandingo man during a segregated fight,
He stood strong and gave his life,
So that we might have the ability to exercise the power of civil rights,
But the last time I took note,
Instead of honoring the dream and registering to vote –
Masses of "so-called brothas" were selling street drugs,
Killing one another and glorifying the game as industry thugs.

Why would you attempt to dictate,
The common ground of your brotherhood –
Based on being victims of hate.
In other words my "nigga;"

Why do you think that we can relate,
Because my flesh has been colored caramel,
Mocha,
Butter pecan,
Or simply brown skin.
I'm African,
And you're American.
I'm free,
And you're a society –
Slave,
Digging your own people's grave,
Fulfilling the plan of the Ku Klux Klan,
Executing the distinction of the black man.

If you chose to remain intellectually suppressed,
Mentally oppressed,
Spiritually possessed,
And emotionally stressed –
I will not be labeled liable,
The truth is, I love all people, but your slave mentality is not
desirable.

The Reformation Of Slavery

My desire is not to be
Racially –
Prejudice.
So I hate to even mention this,
But our black-blood is getting even more distorted,
Because my black brothers have aborted –
Their devotion to the notion,
That there still remains a need for Afro-centric purity,
Unequivocally,
Blackness
Is more than just,
The complexion of dark skin,
It's the heritage of our roots that lies deep within
No other race could ever comprehend,
Unfortunately they can only pretend,
But in the end,
You'll find yourself enslaved all over again.

You call it diversity,
But it's a curse to me,
Because if they don't pollute it,
Than they'll dilute it,
But they'll never salute it,
Because black and white is as different as day and night,
And as much as some people some people don't want to admit it,
We live in a society, which makes it impossible for black folks to
forget it.

Sellouts call me radical,
But reality has labeled me practical.
I embrace every race,
Although they smile in my face,
I know my place,
The Ebonics we speak,
The black history we teach,
The African rhythms we beat,
Nor the soul food we eat,
Will ever become a respected culture in this white society.
But I'm proud of who I am,

And I don't give a "Uncle Sam"
Will not bring me under any other persuasion,
I was born a black man and I will not die thinking like a Caucasian.

No offense my Caucasian friends,
But then again,
I'm from the other side of the railroad tracks,
And for too long have my people been under your attack.

The point of this – is what I don't want you to miss,
Personally –
I think it's a disgrace
For a white woman to stand in a "sista's" place,
I don't mean to put nobody on the spot,
But they see us as brothers whether you like it or not,
And you ought –
To be ashamed
To stand before an altar of sacrifice,
Fail to think twice –
Then give a white woman your stolen slave name.

O' and by the way,
Did I say,
One of my best friends is white,
Isn't that the cliché they always say,
But in regards to this inter-racial plight,
That still doesn't make it right,
But psychologically they've brainwashed us to accept it –
But my mind is strong and I still reject it.

In reality,
Your matrimony,
Was not the unity,
Of two families,
Because the black and white race,
Will never stand face to face,
In true and perfect harmony.
Although I never expect that –
The clear-coated-blue-eyed-white-woman will ever understand,
That she's a thief and a slave master,
Because once again her kind has stolen the black man.

Colorless Realities

Close your eyes and carefully listen,
While I destroy the metaphoric tradition –
Of oral poetry.

Because sometimes I can't see,
The beauty,
Of reality.

Over four hundred centuries,
My people have suffered from emotional injuries,
And now they've locked over fifty percent -
Of our male population in state penitentiaries.

From the slave plantation,
To racial segregation,
Now incarceration –
This has been the journey our black male population.

And even with the sweetest metaphors of poetry,
There seems to be –
No lyrical beauty,
To this colorless reality.

In addition to our forty acre and a mule petition –
For restitution,
During the civil rights movement we fought for an institution –
To the Constitution,
That would give our people true liberty,
Not political charity,
Or institutionalized slavery.

And unfortunately,
You refuse to see,
That the Constitution was not written for you or me.
The statistics of our society –
Best illustrate the government's priority.
And in case you haven't recognized,
Don't be surprised,
When you realize,

That white supremacy,
Was intended to eliminate you and me,
These are just fragments of color blind realities.

Why must a teenager wrestle with the fact,
That he or she is black,
Disrespected by other races,
Rejected in suburban places,
Police chases
And nothing erases –
This psychological infiltration,
Of racial hatred and segregation,
And even though it's unfortunate and should not be,
It's still another colorless reality.

The unspoken word is a representation of life,
A black man's reality unveiled in black and white.

Caramel Colored Sellout

I've been trying
To take your black mind
To another level,
But every since that blue-eyed devil –
Convinced you that I'm the rebel
You turned your back on your true enemy,
And started hawking me,
From the corners of your eyes I see you stalking me.

If your race –
Was a race,
You would be losing,
Because you keep confusing –
The coach with the referee,
Your black mind is still a servant to white society,
Kunta Kinte said,
"Fiddler, how can 'dis' be,
Is you too blind to see,"
Or is this black shell simply too much for you to bear,
So you wear –
Uncle Tom's uniform,
Trying to conform,
To another nationality,
Because you're too weak to be,
A minority –
Individuality,
Isn't even a part of your vocabulary,
And it's very scary –
To think,
That if I blink,
Even for that tenth of a second you won't have my back.

In fact,
That
Might be the very opportunity,
For you to conquer me,
Just like our Sellout African ancestors on the Gold Coast,
You represent the most –
Bitter part of our history

And coincidentally,
You're proud to be –
Without a doubt,
A caramel colored sellout.

Who needs caramel colored police chiefs,
Who are just thieves,
Hidden underneath,
And trapped within
Black skin
Who only pretend –
To be my brother,
And I can't tell the difference between him and the others.

Why must I turn the corners –
Into neighborhoods I never even new exist,
Because I'm trying to resist,
The caramel-colored police who is driving behind me –
Trying to fine me,
Not that four-letter word that ends with a "D",
But F.I.N.E.
They've allowed the black man,
To join the police Klan,
But what I still don't understand,
Is why he keeps selling out to the white man.
They call it "racial profiling,"
But I call it beguiling,
How can I blame white people for the cruel things I see,
Which chocolate-covered people are doing –
Who look just like me,
Caramel colored sellouts invading society.

And it incenses me to see,
Liquor stores across the street –
From black churches which are side by side,
Not even trying to hide,
Their animosity;
Churches infused with bitter hostility –
Yet everybody claims to be,
Religiously –
Minded,

But you've been blinded,
By the simple minded
Messages
Of your self-ordained caramel-colored pastor;
A racial disaster,
Right before the masters –
Eyes.

And yet you lie –
In demise,
And try
To make people believe that you're a spiritual leader,
But you're really a deceiver,
And your church,
Has been cursed.
Because a soul which fails to forgive,
Cannot walk by faith, prosper, or live.

And with this current President we're really in trouble,
Because black folks have forgotten our true struggle,
Now we fight and we toggle –
With each other,
Our sisters and brothers.

Instead of supporting our black leaders,
We watch the white man as he politically beat us –
Down
With words and ridicule our mistakes,
No matter the reality,
Even if it's JJ's adultery –
Never partake in self-hate.

White people gave us a few financial loans,
And now we think we own –
The right.
To arrogantly assume that we're better than –
The next black man.
You better come up with restoration plan,
To revive hope in –
Every African,
Trapped within

These caramel walls made of flesh,
Because as a people we possess –
The ability to change the universe,
But nothing makes our struggle worse,
Than caramel colored sellouts.

The Black Sheep of Society

There's something about life I've rarely recognized,
And to my dismay and insidious surprise,
I've finally realized;
I've been arrogantly hypnotized.
I've made myself believe my own lies,
My black flesh is simply a disguise,
Which hides my vulnerability;
Ashamed of my own identity.

If people could only see –
The real me.
Feel my agony,
Passionately,
The world would be –
A better place,
And maybe love would erase the stereotypes.

I'm like –
Darkness in the still of the night,
Tremendously different, yet my moon still gives light.
Whether my thoughts are wrong or right,
Black or white,
Blind or with sight,
Dark or bright –
I'm different, but still the same.

And it's really deep,
The way they call me the black sheep.
So the media creeps and peeps –
Imposes
And
Exposes –
The scandals in the my neighborhood,
And if they only would –
See my people like the rest of the world;
We're precious pearls.
Still inside the shell –
So it's difficult to tell.

Yet the newspapers search for the skeletons behind our closet doors,
Although, Christ died for all sins, so mine are no different from yours.

Many people still call me out my name,
The word "nigga" has proclaimed my fame.
And what I still cannot explain,
Is how life has forced me to play this challenging game,
I inhale the pain,
My tears fall like midnight rain,
Beating viciously on the windowpanes –
Of my heart.
But I'm satisfied,
And I will no longer attempt to hide –
This brown skin.

I am a black man,
And I will always stand –
With other black sheep.
For I will not cheat –
Myself from walking down the road,
Of the greatest legacy ever told.

Uncle Tom's Great Grandson

I'm not fazed by my urban enemies,
When they speak evil of me,
Their cheap rumors are like free publicity,
Minds are then filled with curiosity.

Just as long as you understand,
That your great grandfather was two strokes short
Of producing a real man or woman
And your cheap profane shots,
Are not –
Even worth,
The black dirt,
Which has been crumbled and scattered
Upon the face of the earth.

When my urban enemies come upon me to eat up my flesh,
They never possess –
The endurance
To influence,
My blood to bubble,
Because my spirit is secretly hidden –
During the time of trouble.

I 'dis' – and do not respect,
In fact, I reject,
The continuity
Of individuals who are filled with childhood like immaturity.
I'm going to charge you with gratuity,
Because for you to hear me vent,
It's worth more than the percent,
Than a five cent –
Fake such as yourself,
Could ever afford to pay,
So stay –
In your place.

Are you two-faced,
Or double-minded,
Or simply blinded

By the fact
That –
Gossip is a double-edged sword,
Be careful, you might cut yourself –
It's not intended to be used whenever you get bored.

Did you think you were destroying my reputation?
Even when I'm joking around –
My subconscious is still in deep concentration,
I win wars exercising biblical meditations.
I understand that you get jealous –
When peripherally,
Your wondering eyes see,
The majority –
Even white society,
Connecting with my personality,
But instead of hating;
Take notes,
And rehearse,
Then start participating.

When you see me,
I'm aware that you see,
A mirror reflection –
Of what your birth parents expected you to be,
So unfortunately,
My mere existence reminds you that you're a failure,
So it's not even necessary for me to open my mouth and tell you.

So I must be your worse,
Living curse.
I'm like a boomerang,
Because without even saying a thing,
I can effect what you do and say.
I'm all in your mind –
I have the power to press
Play, stop, fast-forward or rewind;
I even know when you're telling the truth –
And I know when you're lying.
You're like a hand-puppet without a mind – always crying,
Too bad the Wizard in Oz doesn't really exist,

Because you're like a scare-crow hanging in the mist –
Of a dried-up corn field,
Against your own will.

And you call yourself my "homey,"
If you don't tell –
Then I won't tell,
But we both know you're a phony.

You are one of Uncle Tom's –
Great grandsons.
You are the real reason black folks don't get alone,
You treat your own people wrong;
Hating the culture of your own race,
Bleaching the black skin on your own face,
Trying desperately to erase and replace –
You're Afro-centric identity,
Refusing to accept reality,
You're the epitome of an Uncle Tom,
Hear me when I say, "run 'sellout' run."

CHAPTER IV
That Thing Called Love

This chapter celebrates love. My desire is to poetically document the ups and downs of relationships, from the intimacy and romance to the pain and selflessness. It is my desire that these love poems provide a positive influence for Christian couples. Hopefully, men and women will receive inspiration from the poetic testimonies of others who have experienced both the harshness of loosing love and love's gentle embrace. Much like other traditional love poems, my poetry embraces a smooth, relaxing rhythm that will allow each reader to vividly imagine that invisible silent element called love.

Trying To Explain Love

With many missing words and unexplained abbreviations,
I'm walking along the Atlantic Coast on a summer afternoon –
Trying to explain love.

Like on a hot summer day,
In the middle of May,
While the hot blinding –
Sun is penetrating and shinning,
Then suddenly –
Simultaneously,
It begins to rain.
Love is too difficult to explain,
Like a complicated mind game -
So I've changed my name
To divinity,
Because I want to be,
The first man to travel through heartache and pain,
Then lyrically explain
The reality,
Of this mystical analytical untouchable subject called love.

Love,
I'm trying *oratorically*,
To express metaphorically –
The way I feel about you,
But my thoughts and words are torn in two.

My mind is deep sea diving
Into my inner-man,
My pounding heart is thriving
To get my wet lips to understand,
So that I can release,
A fragmented piece,
Of love in its purest form.
Now my sweaty hands are cold,
And my rushing blood is warm,
The explanation is hidden deep inside of me,
Because apparently –

Love is a deeply buried treasured mystery.
When I open my softly closed eyes I cannot see,
Because underneath my eyelids,
Are tiny bits
Of the definition of love –
Carefully interwove,
Inscribed in the language of meditation,
With many missing words and unexplained abbreviations.

I'm trying to explain love,
Not that tingling sensation called lust or infatuation,
Or the insinuation –
Of the human mind,
But the kind
Of love
That is heard by the deaf,
And seen by the blind.

Small voices echoing in shore shells,
Impels –
My heart to travel the distant,
It takes persistence
To unveil the existence
Of love.

I hear waves evaporating on the rocky coast,
And I'm tasting the most -
Bitter sensations,
My heart is shivering at the sound of sweet vibrations,
Made by the whistling wind as it crackles in my ear,
And I can only hear –
Echoes of Love.

Raindrops falling up above my head
I'm prepared to get wet, but instead
Like virga, the rain sublimes before reaching the ground
I'm in the middle of this desert and there's nothing around
Palm trees and desert heat, sunny skies and mountain peaks
The rapid beat of my racing heart causes the kind of heat
That makes the possibility of love evaporate
But despite the way it seems to dissipate

I'll keep trying to explicate this thing called love.

I see abbreviated words disappearing
And reappearing –
But my tender heart has stopped fearing,
The loss of this pleasant mystery,
Because I am now softly hearing love –
And love is attentively hearing me.

With many missing words and unexplained abbreviations,
I'm walking along the Atlantic Coast on a summer afternoon –
Trying to explain love.

Quiet Expression

There is no need of speechlessly stalling,
When my heart is consistently falling –
For the most desirable woman in the universe,
No other secret could ever be worse,
To conceal what I feel –
Would be an emotional curse.

So today –
In my own poetic way,
I'll unveil –
The mystery,
As my flattering lips tell –
The history,
Of how my heart fell –
Deliriously.

Undeniably,
I'm magnetically attracted to her celestial beauty.
I feel the kind of connection,
That won't allow me to look in any other direction.
Yeah, this thing is "vibing,"
And I'm thriving –
Off her intelligent ambitions,
When she whispers, my tingling ears love to just listen.

My soul has been branded,
And love has demanded –
That I follow my heart,
Beats that never stop –
"Tic Toc, Tic Toc."

Because in this short time
Love has made me so blind,
That my drifting mind –
Has insisted,
That I resist it,
But love is gently and persistently,

Controlling my deepest reality,
Lost and drifting somewhere in infinity.
And my mind is going in circles,
Repeatedly, my heart is jumping hurdles,
Admittedly, I'm in love

I'm no longer confused,
I just don't want to abuse –
Her second impression,
So my thoughts have been concealed,
And to some extent revealed –
Within these quiet expressions.
It's not that easy
To please me
That quickly
But emotionally –
She squeezed out of me,
The commitment to be,
The man that she needs.

I'm caught up in the middle of this emotional world wind,
Falling in love over and over again,
And wondering –
If this time will be,
The prescription for love that will last throughout eternity,
Because forever –
Ends to soon.

Now I'm experiencing pulsating meditations,
I keep contemplating,
Sending signals in telepathic vibrations,
And quietly anticipating –
Waiting,
On time,
To rewind,
So that I can feel these feeling all over again,
Wondering when –
Did I fall in love for eternity?

Romance

There's a mystique difference –
Between seduction and romance,
That's why my midnight skills –
Steals,
Hearts, leaving only one trace of footprints in the sand,
And other brothers cannot stand,
The way I leave them without a chance
After I've redefined –
Romance;
The final hour –
Before your
Deepest fantasy,
Becomes acquainted with virtual reality,
Leaving the mind filled with curiosity.

Romance has very little to do with lovebirds and honeybees,
It's about hot-oil messages on Caribbean Islands –
Underneath tropical palm trees,
Inhaling the moisture of the Atlantic breeze.

It's the gentle-sensual-touch,
Without the lust and sexual rush.
The nibble on the earlobe,
While whispering fairy tales of how one soft kiss –
Changed a royal-prince,
From an undesired toad.

Romance is the delight of knowing,
That you're still going –
To be here when the sunrises,
With no unwanted surprises,
Starring intimately into my brown eyes,
Waiting patiently to explode,
Into the next episode –
Of passion.

Romance –
Is not based on a quick glance,
It's a magnetic force,

Which of course,
Comes from the most powerful source –
Called love.

Romance is the harmony,
Seized within softly-spoken-poetry,
The commitment my lips recite,
Underneath the reflection of an ocean moonlight,
Standing on the Atlantic Coast –
Embracing the most,
Beautiful girl
In the entire world.
Spending time together,
Drinking fine wines together,
And reading between the lines.
Together –
Wherever,
In unity –
Just you and me,
The two of us; alone,
Soaking my gentle-wet kisses –
Into the pours
Of your
Smooth collarbone.

Neck messages and back rubs,
Long bubble baths together –
In rose-pedal-filled-heart-shaped tubs.

The intimacy of passionate French kisses,
Watching falling stars and making unspoken wishes,
Laying underneath,
And feeling the heat –
Of red moons and urban sunsets,
Nothing is as romantic as this.

Enslaved

To me –
Love has many names,
Dear, Distant and Passionate,
Intimate all the same.
I dare not judge between the three,
Least I stumble at my own discretion,
A broken heart has taught me this painstaking lesson.

I once thought love was as –
Soft as a pedal of a fully bloomed rose,
But nobody truly knows,
Unless God speaks,
Then love creeps –
Into your heart.
Because the imagination can be so cunning;
I've seen two hearts running –
In the same direction,
But then one turned at the intersection –
Of life.

Last night –
I was tricked,
By my own thoughts;
Dreams filled with rain,
Represent pleasure leading to pain:
Because
I was,
Carried away on the wings of a longed for fantasy;
Of making love romantically,
And after my morning yarn,
The brutality –
Of this cruel reality,
That I ignored here to fore,
Was no more.
Seeped like a memory,
Quietly –
Through my linen sheets –
Then it creeped,

Through my "pillow's veins,"
Awaken to a fairytale love that never new my real name.

I must have been sinfully stupid,
To have put my faith in the Grecian Cupid,
When God of Greece had a better plan,
But my lust-filled eyes didn't understand.

Butterflies that wouldn't settle,
No answers to life's riddle.
Tears that would not stop falling,
My imagination kept calling –
Out her name,
Very obvious that the pain –
Would not soon go away.
And although with a dagger I thrust therein,
I continued to pretend.
And the hope of what I thought was meant to be,
Was killing me.
In that moment, I wanted to commit suicide
My lies were like acid to my pride
No more dignity
For a man like me
Time was far too spent,
My midnight sins remained content –
Within my heart.
Daggers cannot stop the poison lust starts.

I'm a prisoner in my mind,
I'm blind -
Because only in my daydreams,
Have I seen,
That thing –
Called love.

It's shameful how I was in love "all-by-myself,"
There was no one else.
I painted a picture only I could see,
Mentally –
I saw what was meant to be,
And others saw reality:

A prison picture of only me.

And although God wants what's best for me,
I cannot see.
I live life like –
A fairytale;
Much like Romeo and Juliette,
And I'm willing to bet
The deception
Of my perceptions,
Is leading me to suicide,
Because each day I hide,
Behind the pride –
Of denial.

I must be deceived;
Because I believe,
I keep hearing mating calls,
Behind these heart-shaped prison walls.

Who –
Has ever known a make-believe love like this,
I wished to God;
That this –
Sensation in my heart
Was real –
But still,
My imagination could not capture it,
My deepest fantasy could not rapture it,
And daydreams,
Sometimes they mean
Everything,
But they are but for a moment and cannot seize time.

This magnetic force that I possess deep within my mind,
Makes me feeble –
Each time;
Each time I know you exist,
Your tender touch I will always miss;
Emotionally
And

Mentally –
I've become a servant to this.
For such I cannot replace,
Or erase –
No matter how hard I try,
Sin has no eyes,
Therefore, slaves cry.

Sinful

EVERY TUESDAY,
Freaky Ruby –
Would seduce me.

During the late night hours she abused me,
She never teased me,
But what confused me –
Was how cheating Ruby,
Was never satisfied,
With the man she had.

Maybe his...
Was too small,
Or he didn't sex her from behind –
With her face smashed against the wall,
Or maybe he didn't make her crawl –
Around the room,
But then again,
Ruby never liked a man who came too soon.

You see, Ruby was a freak,
One night every week,
We would sneak
And grind cheek to cheek,
And I never made a creamy mess –
Because Ruby would swallow - Unless,
She decided
To try it
All over her face,
Or she'd have me release in another place.

But truthfully,
Horny Ruby,
Did not belong to me.
I was her sex machine,
Emotional our little escapades didn't mean a thing,
It was just a weekly routine.

Every Tuesday
Ruby showed me
Her legs were double jointed,
It was like her entire body was anointed –
To bump and grind,
Upside-down in action, on top and from behind,
If I named it – she didn't mind,
And I wasn't ashamed of it – so we took our time.

Upon layers of sweat,
Engraved all over her body I could see my fingerprints,
Body heat was our only cover,
As her fuzzy tongue discovered,
A planet called Mandingo

Every Tuesday
Ruby reminded me of a professional,
There wasn't a thing about sin that she didn't know.

Being that she was married,
We secretly carried,
Our sex affair –
Elsewhere.

Iron chains, hands cuffs and fake finger nail tips,
Body piercings and leather whip -
cream,
and everything -
that priest call perverted.
Chocolate covered condoms and metal vice-grips,
Firm breast, a fuzzy tongue and nice thick hips,
These were just a few of the tools,
That we used –
To infuse,
The ecstasy
Between Ruby and me.

Upon the conclusion
Of my demonic confusion,
I was drenched in sin;
A servant of fornication.

I was so caught up in the physical pleasure,
That my soul failed to spiritually measure,
The fact
That
Every Tuesday,
I wasn't simply given in
To the will of sin,
I was intimately sleeping,
With the second daughter of the devil,
I'd taken sin to a completely different level –
Called AIDS,
And now that my disease has reached its final stage,
My soul will receive an eternal wage;
For the wages of sin is death.
This is why I'll soon be left –
Behind and blind,
Because I refused to find –
The discipline,
To the stop the sin,
Which had taken total control –
Of my body, spirit and lust-filled soul.

Duplicating Dialects

I'm trying to paint like Picasso,
But you're making duplicates,
Before I even finish the original.

Every time
I paint a line
I find –
That you keep lying,
Are you trying
To confuse my long strokes,
In the minds of other folks.

Even though you knew the
Answer was B,
You still circled C,
Because you wanted to be a
Duplicate of Mona Lisa.

A duplicate is only a refraction,
It's never the center of attraction,
It's void of intimacy,
And I'm not impressed,
Because it's been processed,
And it wasn't strokes by me.

I could have fainted,
When Michael Angelo painted,
Abstract black and white tongues tied,
I'm trying to hide,
The way your tongue slides –
In backbiting motions of trivial talk,
But this portraits reflects the expression
That your lying tongue walks,
Across canvases
And dances
With the devil,
Angelo was a rebel,
His legacy is that he sculptured reality –
On a completely different level.

For your final performance,
I see an enormous
Artistic stage.
Wait a minute turn the page,
Better yet –
I see rattlers prepared to engage,
Rembrandt's wrist was filled with rage
When he painted
Tainted
Seductive lip prints and oratorical excursions,
Bright colors merging,
Rumors and gossip stirring.

The red velvet draped curtains began to rise,
I couldn't believe my eyes –
It was a Kandinski,
The epitome
Of artistic ability;
Name-calling
Tears falling
And yet your tongues keeps crawling
Across the canvas,
On the flip side Kandinski painted your last chance,
But no matter what,
Your rattling tongue would not shut up.

Your tongue is wrecking my flow,
I'm trying to paint like Picasso,
But you're making duplicates,
Before I even finish the original.

Rhythm-less Blues Of Divorce

She was my oxygen,
But jealously knocked and then,
She left a *brotha* breathless.

She was my harmony,
Until she brought harm to me,
And now there's no beat in me –
She even stole the rhythm from my blues.
I'm trapped behind the bars of
Accusations, assumptions and strange notions,
My pounding heart is pulsating in irregular motions.

My whole world has been torn apart,
Because from the start,
She was as gentle as –
The moonlit reflection upon the Egyptian Nile,
She possessed a style –
That could make a blind "brotha" see planet Jupiter,
During a blizzard storm in the month of December,
My tongue discovered every inch,
As she had me speaking French –
In sign language all over her brown skin,
But then again,
If you would -
Let me explain this so that it will be,
Unequivocally
Eternally understood;
She was my May flower,
Budding in a far away place,
Where outer space –
Meets eternity and time no longer exist,
She was the kind of *sista* eyes could not resist.

I was amazed,
When I first gazed –
Into her dark brown eyes,
But like a blind man, I did not realize,
That she was wearing a disguise.
Didn't know that sin could hide –

Behind flesh so tender.
But soon she had me feeling like an offender;
A wife abuser and a deadbeat father,
I asked myself, "Why even bother;"
Working on this relationship –
She was worse than a 3-day roadtrip.
The police took a report from my lying spouse,
Then the sheriff escorted me in and out my own house.
Allowing me to get clothes and shoes
I felt like fool that had been emotionally used
Secretly,
She –
Devised a plan for me,
And I was caught by the surprise,
Mesmerized by all her evil lies,
As she tried –
To hypnotize;
The white man in the black robe into believing,
That in her psychotic disposition she was worthy of receiving,
All of my possessions,
She lost the case – but still didn't learn her lesson.
When she slowly surrendered her left hand into the air,
And stated, "I swear –
To tell the truth."
The judge's only concern was the two youth.

Sweat dropped as I wondered, "What will he do?"
As a black man,
I was aggravated,
Because underneath her right hand,
Her lying heart pulsated,
And everybody in the room could tell,
As she stared,
An evil glared –
With a reflection from hell.

The epitome of all that she did to me,
Is when she unsuccesfully tried to take my seed from me,
Had me tossing and turning with a *sista* named Grieve,
Because my mind and body needed the kind of relieve –
That I sought in the bottle labeled *Turning Leaf,*

Relaxing my mind,
With fine red and white wines,
Wondering if in time –
I'll ever trust like that again.

I lived life as my son's hero and my daughter's first love
Raising my children as a single dad was all I thought of
And now that they've succeeded
I have the joy that I needed to heal
But it's difficult to forget how the pains of divorce feel.

So, I'm trying to focus on God,
But hurt makes it hard,
And the pain that I feel –
Seems so tangibly real.
Soon it'll just be a memory
I refuse to live vicariously
Through the Blues of history.

There was once no rhythm nor harmony in this life of mine,
Because my x-wife used all of her resources, energy and time,
To tamper with my base,
So I had to erase –
And soon I'll replace
The whole sound track.

Love And Pain

I'm thinking thoughts
Gazed –
With the haze,
Of bad memories,
Thoughts of you and me,
That I'm trying to erase,
So that I can chase,
After other thick women with curves –
Who are giving -
Me the respect a man truly deserves.

But I keep reflecting –
And directing,
My thoughts off yesterday.
The way –
We had so many ups and downs,
Our love was growing by leaps and bounds,
But the things you expected of me,
I rejected -
You see,
Through the years I've suffered tremendous
Pain,
Only to gain –
Frien-enemies who only scandalized my name.
(Frien-enemies are enemies who pretend to be friends with me).

So I've decided to be my own man,
But you couldn't seem to understand –
So you nicked and picked at the choices I made –
Dug your own grave,
Turn the page –
Of our relationship,
To a chapter entitled rage,
So now the stage –
Was set up,
For a break up.

This is my explanation,
And I don't care about the insinuations,

That other people make.

Sometimes I try not to remember,
But this has been a cold December,
So I'm sitting here, trying to erase –
Memories of you and me;
Burning old pictures in the fireplace,
Trying desperately to forget your beautiful face.
Since it was only a mask
That served the task of deceiving me.

Love and pain,
Go together like clouds and rain.
But what was I thinking of;
I always felt the pain, and you always felt the love.

I still think about your womanly stride,
But I've decided to hide –
My emotions,
Because my soul is tired of the commotion –
That I have to face,
To replace,
This empty space,
In my lonely heart.

From the start -
You were my everything.
But your tongue started rattling,
You were expecting material things,
And my mind started wondering and imagining –
So I decided to close this masquerade book,
And take a closer look –
At another author –
I wish true love could have made what we had perfect –
We would still be together,
Storming the whether,
Breaking every curse,
For better or for worse.

Love Changes

Tonight I'm traveling on the broken pieces of my heart,
This search for love is tearing my soul apart.
Love can be dangerous,
Because it changes –
Sometimes rearranges,
Like a hurricane,
It causes so much pain,
In the strangest ways.
But it never pays,
When *sistas* attempt to play,
With a brother like mine emotions.
Erupting commotion,
Like flaming lava, let me break this down to you in slow motion.

She wanted to be wined and dined,
She expected my money and my time,
Gold diggers are never satisfied,
They want your checkbook, your black book and your pride,
And if you give her a long stem rose,
She'll expect you to kneel and propose,
Nobody knows –
The mind of a material queen,
Understand what I mean,
One minute she'll want everything,
And in the next minute -
To a material girl love won't mean a thing.

You can –
Commit sin
And caress her until her soft-body screams from within,
You can –
Live right,
And read her poetry at midnight –
Underneath a full moonlight,
But when the clock strikes –
Twelve,
She'll still argue, fuss and fight.
Brothas am I right or am I right.
This is why love can be dangerous,

Because it changes,
Sometimes rearranges,
In the strangest ways.

Then you have those women who don't realize,
That it's more to love than what's between their thighs,
And even though she'll be wearing a disguise,
Her makeup,
Is just a cover-up,
The spirit of Jezebel will always corrupt.
I'm telling you the games people play,
You've got to pay attention to things women say.

Listen as I tell –
Of my first date from hell,
When I first gazed into her moonlit eyes,
I did not realize –
She only wanted to still my sanity,
And humiliate my manly humanity.
I once thought her presence,
Represented the very essence,
Of everything –
Love could ever mean,
I just knew she was my eternal queen.
The jewel of my Nile,
But after a while,
Those
Feelings
Faded.

This is why love can be dangerous,
Because it changes,
Sometimes rearranges,
In the strangest ways.
Openly busted -
And her face looked disgusted.
She was a player and I was her little secret made manifest.
Should I tell the rest,
Or save the best –
For later.

I've never been a hater or a procrastinator,
But she was hiding her feelings between the lines,
Trying to play with my emotions and my mind,
Indeed she was fine,
But I wasn't interested in wasting my time –
On a relationship,
That flipped –
Into a downward psychological spiral,
Soon to emotionally cycle,
To an abrupt end,
A relationship too starved to comprehend.

So I sent her back to tell all her girl friends,
That night I represented for all men,
Although I gave in to lust and sin,
I called out another woman's name,
The third time I came –
In the name of revenge,
I was certainly off the hinge,
Sinking into sin.
My life was being taken by force
I repented and God placed me back on the course.

Yet, I bet she'll never forget –
Love can be dangerous,
Because when the script flips it changes,
Sometimes like boomerangs it rearranges,
In the strangest ways,
But it never pays,
When people attempt to play,
And throw fiery darts
At the precious hearts,
Of the children of God.

I've Finally Discovered Love

I'm remembering intimacy.
The way things use to be,
But I'm tasting bitterness,
Because the thought of this –
Has got me daydreaming,
About the true meaning –
Of love.

Don't now what I was thinking of,
When I allowed you to just walk away.
I should have begged you to stay,
But the pride of my strong –
Masculine manhood got in the way.

So today,
I'm trying to imagine the two of us,
Communication and Trust,
Together
Forever.
No, wait –
Eternity,
Has never sound better to me.

Now I'm wondering,
If you'll take me back
In fact,
I'm determined to be,
The man you first so in me,
Tenderly –
Touching your sensitivity.

The reality;
Is that I'm breathless without you,
And don't know what I'm going to do,
Without a woman like you –
As my life support,
So please don't abort,
The thought of us,
Forgive my melancholy drops of lust

And trust,
That I'll be satisfied.

I'm passionately tasting
The fragrance of your presence,
How did I overlook your essence?
I've discovered that this love was true,
And now I don't know what I'm going to do,
About this love I've veiled only for you.

Feel me screaming,
As my eyes are closed tightly;
My body is coming –
In your direction.
My arms are stretched-out,
And I feel you running –
Back to me.

Please try an understand, my plan for eternity;
I'm kneeling and asking –
For your tender hand, again and again, in matrimony.
I've finally discovered love.

CHAPTER V
Behind The Stained Glass

It's strange how Christians represent the temple of God, and yet I'm seldom able to make the parallel between many people involved in church and those who share a relationship with God. This chapter highlights very sensitive poetry. It speaks of things I've personally experienced during my Christian walk dealing with religious people. Each poem in this chapter unveils my personal thoughts, the position of my heart, my prayers, my likes and dislikes concerning that which is most important to me – my own spiritual experience. Throughout this book I've shared portions of myself with each reader; however, this chapter takes people into the secret place of my heart. This chapter unveils the depths and disposition rarely seen or heard by those who are not in my inner-circle. Throughout this book I've used words to paint images within the human imagination. This chapter reflects more than well-arranged metaphors, but moreover it takes the human heart into a realm behind the stained glass of my spiritual experience. I pray that the Word, which has gone unspoken in your life, is made manifest in this chapter. May you see Christ; experience Him, know Him, share Him, love Him – for He is the Word made flesh. Until you come to the knowledge of the Son of God, your life will continue to revolve around the bitter and sweet episodes of *The Unspoken Word*.

The Choir Director

Let us turn to Revelation 12:4.
She is the choir director,
Sisters in the church do not respect her,
Carnal minded brothers can't reject her,
And her own mother does not accept her.

She teaches the brotherhood's new member class,
And the men aren't official members until they pass.

She's a Jezebel,
Always raising hell,
Many people are under her spell,
The preacher can't even tell.
She was vindictive, seductive, manipulative,
And on a mission,
To cause division.

Listen;
If you think you've never seen a demon before,
Look no more,
Hell's greatest whore,
Has just walked through the door,
And Lucifer,
Is pimpin' her.
In his black brim with the red feather,
And sometimes he wears a robe of his own
Because he hides behind the pulpit his tail is unknown.

He was so cunning and clever –
He's been around forever
So, she didn't even know the enemy she befriended,
Because he used the pleasures of sin and pretended,
To be her best friend,
Let the church say Amen.

Underneath that choir-robe,
The deacon's bucked eyes told –
That she was barely wearing anything,
Sing choir, sing –

Is what the old men said,
After the announcer read,
"Now we'll have an A and B selection from our choir,"
The brothers stood and clapped filled with lust and desire.

She looks straight into your eyes,
Then she'll hypnotize you with what's between her thighs,
And don't think for a moment,
That she's not your opponent,
After you've been allured by it,
There's no cure for it;
That thing called lust –
Must,
Be one of the devil's greatest tools,
Effective on fools,
Who fail to listen to sound advice.
The lust of the eye, lust of the flesh and the pride of life.

You better think twice,
Because her intent is to drain you,
From the substance that sustains you.

Your soul has just been date rapped,
And your biggest mistake,
Was when you thought you could take –
Coals up your bosom and not be burned,
And you still haven't learned,
Because she-devil has turned –
Your back on Yahweh,
I thought I told you.

When you loose your desire for her,
She'll still be the choir director,
And your soul will be lost,
Because there's always a cost –
To take a trip,
On the strip,
Then sip,
From the tip,
Of sin.
Amen.

False Prophets

Love me from a distance –
I don't need any extra pain,
You lie to people in their faces,
Speak evil of their names in vain.

You're like a stray-female dog without a master,
Your life is one great disaster –
So you agitate the wombs of others,
Viscously backbite your sisters and brothers.

You have the low-life signs of a bastard child,
Or maybe I simply don't like your style –
The way you grin
And then,
Rare back –
With a sudden attack.
Like the serpent that I hate,
You're identical to a snake,
The way you slither and slide,
Humiliate people's pride,
And then you hide –
Behind the same old façade,
After you've squeezed –
And seized –
The hope out of another victim's heart.

Love me from a distance,
You have a destructive persistence,
Therefore, I'm exercising resistance.

You must flee,
According to the divine law and principality.
Start mourning,
Because this is your final warning
I'm destroying everything you represent,
I've been sent –
To reveal your hidden identity.

You claim to possess the ability –

To speak prophecy,
But your words never come to pass,
You speak riddles amazingly fast,
Making it difficult for young Christians to grasp –
Your true identity;
And it's really deep,
Because you're disguised as the perfect sheep
but really –
You're the enemy:
A product of the anti-Christ,
And your big mistake,
Is that you imitate
the Christ.
The one who you really hate,
So you've become his fake;
This is a Face Off.

Because all fake pastors,
God's been watching you,
And I'm confronting you,
And shinning the light from glory on the things you do.
I've felt the pain of God's children you manipulate,
That's another thing I hate,
The way you use people sins
And pretend –
As if they're less than you.
You've hidden the wrongs you do;
"If any man says he is without sin he is a lie,"
And this is the very reason why –
I can see straight through your cunning facade,
It's not very hard.

I am the ready writer;
And God's Word has spoken it,
So with this pen –
I've seen your expected end,
And I've written it with the tongue of prophecy,
And you do not have the ability,
To hide from the judgment of your iniquity.

You're cursed,

With the worst –
Kind of disease,
And unfortunately,
You will soon pay the penalty.
Because you're a false prophet,
And the final judgment will soon stop it.

I Am Flesh

Desperately trying to disengage,
The sinful rage –
That causes my soul to surrender.

I am the great pretender;
A hypocrite,
Because I tell fragmented bits –
Of reality.
I hide my weaknesses behind my masculinity.

My secret sins are plenty,
Far too many –
To confess
So I've become obsessed and possessed
With my own public identity.
I've forsaken sensitivity,
I've ignored human dignity
Failed to focus on my own inabilities,
Made a mockery of other people's insecurities,
And made life all about me.

I'm sending mixed mess
And stress.
I chase waterfalls,
Other names I call –
To distract and deflect my own shame.
I play manipulating mind games.

Although my sins are the same,
I think I'm better than others so I point the blame –
It's common for me to inflict emotional pain,
Because my tongue I cannot tame,
Then when others complain,
I fail to completely explain –
The whole truth
I specialize in distorting the minds of youth.

I think the Lord is my Shepard yet I still want,
Deep within –

I am wanting sin.
I tell rhetorical stories –
So that I can get the glory.
Why must I chase brooks and streams
When he leads me beside the still waters.

I am my own enemy,
And I do not have the ability
To conquer –
Self;
I am flesh.

Crystal Clear Closet Doors

I read your thoughts,
And it's not my fault –
That you've been caught.

I'm just wondering why,
You've chosen to live this hypocritical lie.

You're the author of a make believe reality;
You've been living in a den of iniquity,
Afraid that other people will see –
The real you.

Didn't know that I could see straight through,
Your crystal clear closet doors.
I've seen your intimate affairs of unprotected sex,
I've watched your mind become perplexed –
Trying to recall the lie you were living yesterday.

If these white walls –
Could call,
Out your name,
You'd still try to redirect the blame.

Not only that,
But as a matter of fact,
You've got secrets that I'm afraid to tell,
All liars shall have their part in hell –
Because God chooses not to recognize your many identities,
Nor your ever-changing personalities.

If God could not see;
And you had the ability,
Undoubtedly –
You would diligently try,
To tell God a miserable lie –
Pretending and sending,
An untruthful message
To try to cheat your way into the gates of paradise.

Your life is a paradigm of diminishing time
A paradox of *what not's* written between the lines
To call your life a paradise would be a crime –
Nothing about your existence sublime.

You don't even listen to your own advice,
Because when you think twice,
Your mind gets confused,
By the first lie you used,
To explain the same situation.

Looking through your,
Crystal clear closet door,
I've seen you looking at the caller I.D. and procrastinating,
Seen you watching pornography while masturbating,
Seen you lie with the intent of perpetrating,
Seen you trying to cover up your own sinful secrets,
By insinuating –
Negativity about those who surround you,
So that others will not frown on you.

I've seen you sneaking,
Creeping,
And peeping,
In places that you claimed didn't exist,
But the real you could not resist –
Your secret fetishes.

Who do you think you are fooling,
What do you think you are proving.
I've seen through your –
Clear closet door,
It's like a crystal ball,
And you live in a world –
Where Truth means nothing at all.

Walk Out On Water

Fear has assassinated
And dictated
So many hopes and dreams
Turned African kings
Into Egyptian slaves
Buried good ideas in pyramids and six-foot-deep-graves
Because so many other countries were afraid
To step out on the sea
The fear of failing to become
What they've always wanted to be
So the human mind
Has a prideful design
That makes excuses
And uses
Tiny particles of dirt and sand
To stand
On dry land
But if you ever plan
To go beyond the boundaries of the human mind
This is your time
To walk out on water
And faith will take you farther
Than you've ever been
Undoubtedly
It's about time for me
To do the unthinkable
My faith is unsinkable
The souls of my feet are walking on the ocean and the sea
Treading faithfully
I'm the statue of declaration for spiritual liberty
And fear is no longer stopping my ability,
I see Christ standing on the other side of the sea,
I hear His voice saying, "Come to me."

The Wings Of Love

Child of God,
Don't give your body to burned,
Until you've learned –
This lesson about to teach,
And I hope it'll reach –
To the depths of your soul,
Because everybody needs to know –
What love is.

Far beyond any treasured conception,
The imagination –
Could ever completely retrieve,
Deep within the essence of spirit –
Hidden within faith; things not quite conceived.

Love is more than just some invisible force,
But of course –
Being that you're a child of God,
And His Spirit dwells within your heart,
Sarcastically speaking – you knew that,
But never faced the facts.
That's why when the devil is raising hell,
It's not that difficult for us to tell –
Christians who really know what love is.

Love is the part of you that tries to understand,
When mortal man,
Smile in your face,
And speaks lies behind your back –
And other childhood-insignificant-silly things like that.

Simply because we are spiritual kings and queens,
We're going to suffer many things.
And It'll be easy to love your family and friends because they love
you too,
But the true test of love is with your enemies who can't stand you.

Christ rose to give us everlasting life,
And yet we stab one another with words like knives.

He died because he love me,
And although you lie - it doesn't bother me,
Because he set me free.
And yet you claim to understand this mystery –
Called love.

Love is more than just some invisible force,
But of course –
Being that you're a child of God,
And His Spirit dwells within your heart,
Sarcastically speaking – you knew that,
But never faced the facts.
That's why when the devil is raising hell,
It's not that difficult for us to tell –
Christians who really know what love is.

You must recognize –
That the devil's demise,
Is his device,
To disguise and deceive,
Everyone that believes –
In love.

Love is more than just an inner feeling,
It will draw you if you're willing.
Stop concealing what you're feeling,
God's revealing –
The mystery of love.

It overcomes the bitterest emotions,
Eliminates the tantalizing commotion,
Flows like the waves of the ocean,
Hypnotizes the soul like a potion –
The Spirit of God moves only by this notion,
Not by power or by might –
Loves makes that which is wrong, right.

True love –
Is a treasure trove,
Which can interwove,
All of our hearts together.

We are a family of believers,
Our enemy is the deceiver,
So as we run this spiritual race,
Everyone must maintain their individual pace,
But in the end –
We will all come out together
Glorious and victorious.

Soul Warrior

Grace is sufficient to combat sin,
And if you truly love God,
You'll try your best not to do it again.

Understand that your worst enemy is sin,
Because it will slowly kill your spirit within,
Yet always pretend to be your friend.

I'm describing a poison that taste like sugar and spice,
Sin is an evil hiding behind things soft and nice,
Although the wages of sin bears a very costly price.

The wages of sin is death,
But the gift of God is life,
So sin will make you think that you just can't do what's right.

Sin has an eternal plan,
A diabolical deception is something difficult to comprehend,
Angels fell from heaven to hell – because they didn't understand,
But Russian roulette will certainly kill a man.

Oftentimes you can't see sins' face,
But it will leave you with a scar you won't be able to erase.

Sin is an invisible force,
That'll take your carnal mind on a course;
You think she's your best friend,
But he is really the father of sin.
Trying desperately to separate you from humanity,
By attacking your sanity.

Be quiet and pay close attention,
Then notice how your friend fails to ever mention -
Christ.

Sin has no friends.
Sin specializes in the ability to pretend.
It will make you think you're happy when you're really sad inside.
It will make itself your master and humiliate your pride.

It can make you a superstar,
But you won't know who you are.
It will make you forget the power of grace then point the blame,
It will fill you with guilt and change your name.

Sin will chain you to a fantasy -
And anchor you to the belly of hell.
It will capture you into the devil's spell.
Forsake it now -
Or time will tell.
Before you close your eyes
And open your thighs.
Protect yourself and be sure -
That your -
Not sleeping with that friend.
Without abstinence,
There is no confidence –
Of everlasting life.
Because at the moment you least expect,
I suspect;
My friend,
Your life will abruptly come to an end.

Like an illness causing you to lose your sight,
Now you only see darkness -
But you use to walk in the light.

Sin is AIDS and cancer,
Because there is no answer -
Or cure,
To make a man or woman pure,
After they've tasted of the forbidden tree.
But the darkness of death has made you too blind to see.

Shall we continue in sin that grace may abound,
Even though -
We know,
Sin will tear our spirits down.

The Master is coming like a thief in the night,
You better guard your life -

From your fake friends;
Called "Iniquity and Sin."

It wasn't long ago I had a so called friend named sin,
And I never want to see that deceiver again.
Sin stole everything my Heavenly Father gave me,
Sin cunningly tried to enslaved,
Sin even dug a spiritual grave for me.

Sin hung out in my closet far too long,
I even started hating what was right and loving what was wrong.
I was one prayer away from being reprobate,
But it's never too late -
To accept the blame,
And call on the only name -
That can free us.

Soul Warrior,
Stand up for right,
And fight a good fight.
Take up your shield of faith,
Because that's the substance the serpent hates.
Take up your sword, which is the Word,
And put on the helmet of salvation,
This victory calls for a celebration.

God gives a warning before destruction,
We have a choice between life and corruption,
And even though I had a whole lot of sin in me,
I chose life and His grace made me free.

And now I'm singing -
Amazing grace
How sweet the sound,
That saved a wretch like me,
I once was lost,
But now I'm found,
I was spiritually blind,
And constantly lying – to myself,
But now I see.

The Secret Place

Last night
While dreaming in black and white,
I experienced a melancholy
Virtual reality,
As the rhythmic beat of my heart fluttered in slow motion,
I stood meditating on the white crystal sands
Of what looked like the Atlantic Ocean.
I was dreaming serenity,
With such passionate intensity.

I was outside of my body,
My soul was free,
And my thoughts were in harmony –
With eternity.
I was dreaming celestial tranquility.

At first it was noiseless,
Until I started hearing these echoing voices,
My melancholy experience came to an end,
My eyelids crept open and the nightmare began.

I was forced on this course,
Society set the pace,
I never asked to run in this race,
When I was born – the totality
Of this cruel reality slapped me in the face.
But I took it like a soldier,
I thought I told you,
Every time I close my eyes,
Reality cannot deny,
That I escape into a world of visions
Illuminated by my imagination,
Because I'm on a mission
And my dreams are unequivocally the elimination –
Of this expeditious course,
That I've been
Forced
To face
On a daily basis.

Last night
While dreaming in black and white,
I took –
A quick look,
A sneak peak,
At the way life was meant to be,
God's intent I see.
Then very abruptly,
In the blink of an eye it suddenly –
Appeared to me,
That if I live within the restraints of my own reality,
I'd possess the totality –
Of self-control,
Liberty, peace and harmony would anchor my raging soul.

My wretched flesh will soon crumble into dirt,
Because everyday sin gets worse –
And I cannot reverse
The curse
Of birth
On earth,
Sometimes it hurts,
So bad –
And I'm so glad
To say goodbye,
And close my eyes,
As I hail the most high,
Death is signified –
By the empty crystal balls
Called
Deep hallow eyes,
But my soul is experiencing eternal life.
And yet the turmoil I've faced,
Time on earth will never erase,
But since the Savior died in my place,
Surely I'll find eternal peace in the secret place.

(Selah)

My soul is hidden under the shadow of the Almighty.

Found Kneeling Alone

My invisible soul is no longer lost,
My bare feet are positioned before the rugged cross,
I am kneeling alone –
Before the great-white throne,
For I am spirit,
And His voice is like the sound of rushing waters –
Clearly I can hear it.

This is the one thing I've always desired,
To inquire –
In the secret place,
His glory veils His holy face,
I am saturated in His saving grace,
My sins have been forever erased.

I am experiencing the only true intimacy,
The holy One has total control of me,
And yet my soul has never known such liberty.

My human dignity,
Is simply –
The moonlit shadow of His sovereignty,
Eternity –
Has crowned Him with deity.

As I continue to kneel,
I can intimately feel –
The tears falling.
My spirit is consistently calling –
On the name of the Most High.

His presence alone caused my entire countenance to change,
As I kneeled I knew I'd never be the same.
I am worshipping,
And thanksgiving –
In the holy sanctuary,
My iniquities have been buried,
Underneath the soil of the cross that He carried –
On Calvary

He has given me a new desire,
And rescued my soul from drowning daily in flaming fires.
I live in eternity with the King of kings,
I've mounted up like an eagle with angels' wings.

All of this;
Is because
My fainting soul was –
Found kneeling alone.

www.ingramcontent.com/pod-product-compliance
Lightning Source LLC
Chambersburg PA
CBHW071553040426
42452CB00008B/1162